# Their Corner of a Foreign Field

**Peter Clark**

# Their

# Corner

# of a

# Foreign

# Field

ISBN 1 900038 50 1

Published & Printed
by

## GLEN GRAPHICS

4 Ryecroft Park, Wooler, Northumberland NE71 6AS
info@glengraphics.co.uk
www.glengraphics.co.uk

# Contents

## FOREWORD BY AIR VICE-MARSHAL A F C HUNTER CBE AFC DL

Peter Clark's latest book, like its predecessors, is painstakingly researched and compellingly written. He paints a poignant picture of lives given in the cause of freedom and of the last resting places of young men from distant parts of the globe. His account of the circumstances of each fatal accident makes gripping reading and his analysis of the general circumstances and causes of such losses is shrewd and well presented.

It is hard for an airman of a later, peacetime generation to comprehend the obstacles and hazards facing the young crews of the 1940s. Almost to a man, they were woefully inexperienced. They took to the air in aircraft that were primitive by today's standards, difficult to handle, often temperamental and notoriously unforgiving. Under the pressures of war, they flew in terrible conditions and often in the pitch darkness of the blackout. They had few of the aids without which later generations would not consider operating.

The courage of these young men is writ large on the pages of Peter Clark's sensitive account of their paths to distant graves in the lovely countryside where they now lie. He is to be congratulated, not only for the quality of his research, but for having produced a fine memorial to their sacrifice in the cause of the freedom that is now so often taken for granted.

# ACKNOWLEDGEMENTS

Had it not been for Jack Deeble's question regarding the fate of a Canadian Naval Airman with whom he had served in World War II, then the large number of Commonwealth and exiled airmen who are buried in the Borders would not have come to my attention. So it is Jack who not only gets my thanks for initially stimulating my interest in the subject, but also for providing original and unseen material regarding that airman.

Dr Annie Huisman-van-Bergen contributed a large amount of background material in connection with Flying Officer J.W. van Hamel and additionally, via Mrs Grace Grootshoff-van-Hamel, helped to source most of the photographs of that airman. This help, together with her constant enthusiasm and encouragement are much appreciated.

In many cases the only information that was publicly available about the airmen was what appeared on the Commonwealth War Graves Commission headstone. I was able to glean much more information from the CWGC Database via the Internet, and am indebted to Jim Corbett for carrying out this task on my behalf. Jim was also a great help when pinpointing the precise location of some of the incidents.

Many archive centres and official record offices across the world were visited or contacted and the staff at these establishments never cease to earn my gratitude for their efficiency, patience and cheerfulness. Amongst these are Teresa Mailey at the Scottish Borders Archive and Local History Centre, Selkirk, Stephanie Boyd, Sonia Sherman and Michael Wenke at the National Archives of Australia and Mrs Lynly Yates and Mrs Marjorie Crabtree at the Personnel Archives of the New Zealand Defence Force. And, of course, the staff at the Public Record Office, Kew, also warrant my appreciation just for simply doing their job so well.

Occasionally archives available in the public domain failed to reveal all the facts needed to tell a complete story. My only recourse then was to ask the Air Historical Branch of the Ministry of Defence for their help. They were always as helpful as regulations regarding the divulging of confidential material allow them to be. In respect of information from this source I am particularly indebted to Les Morrison who patiently fielded all my enquiries.

An ex-Beaufighter Wireless Navigator, Arthur Harris, who was posted to 132 OTU at East Fortune before being transferred to 79 OTU Nicosia, provided much of the background material regarding that particular aircraft. There is no replacement for anecdotal tales of actual "hands on" experience of a situation, so I am particularly grateful to Arthur for his input. Additionally he also took on the task of proof reading the final script and so I have even more cause to be thankful to him.

What started as a passing interest in an event of long ago eventually led Keith Davies to contact the family of the young airman involved. His tenacity in doing so impressed me greatly and I am extremely grateful to him for allowing me to use the information he received from them.

The Glendale Group of Creative Writers has given me support, encouragement and suggestions as to the format of the guide and indeed their constructive criticism has probably improved the finished product to a point where, hopefully, it has become readable!! One of its members, Susan Veitch, was also responsible for the design of the cover, and gains my admiration for producing this from the very sparse ideas I gave her.

Unfortunately Julie Jones drew the "short straw", but has coped admirably with deciphering my not so legible scrawl and converting it to print.

As usual the publishers have supported me in this venture and without them you would not be reading this.

Lastly, and certainly not leastly, I must thank my friends and family in general, and Chris , my wife in particular for their help and support but mostly patience throughout the production of the guide but especially when work was not proceeding quite as I would have liked.

# INTRODUCTION

There can be little doubt that the Scottish Border country ranks as one of the most scenically beautiful areas of the British Isles. Not only does it have a remote rural picturesqueness, but also the majestic grandeur of the Cheviot Hills and the Southern Uplands. The fact that the lush farm land of the wide river valleys stand cheek-by-jowl with the harsh hills in which those same rivers rise, makes it almost unique in character. But perhaps its strongest attraction is that it seems to be almost totally unspoilt and that time has come to a standstill, the advances of our modern world seemingly having passed it by.

So unspoilt and unchanged, in fact, that were one of its inhabitants from the turn of the 19th Century to return, he would have little trouble in finding his way around, as all the landmarks he would have known still exist, largely in almost unaltered form. It is true that there would be additional new houses and farm buildings, but as they represent such a small fraction of the total, then the hypothetical visitor from a past era should have little trouble in understanding where he was.

He may, however, have a great deal more difficulty in explaining and comprehending the serried rows of pristine white Portland stone headstones, which are present in a number of cemeteries in the area. Why are these graves here, their markers complete with military type badges, the inscriptions on them informing us that those interred below were all young men with a military rank and mostly from foreign climes?

This guide attempts to tell who these men were, and why they are laid to rest in this remote and beautiful place. It is an intensely sad story, but also one of courage, self-sacrifice, and the youthful urge to serve one's fellow men. It chronicles only the stories of those young men from the Dominions and Colonies of the British Commonwealth, and those from countries which were under German occupation during the second World War.

It does not include the seventeen Luftwaffe airmen who are buried at Chevington. This is not through any lingering animosity against Germans or Germany, but solely because of the difficulty in locating any details relating to the service careers of these men.

The guide covers the cemeteries at Chevington near Broomhill,

Kirknewton just north-west of Wooler, Fogo on the Greenlaw to Duns road and Duns.

It also includes an airman not buried in the area, but who is commemorated individually within the area of the guide.

# GLOSSARY OF TERMS

Throughout the guide a number of types of RAF (or RAAF, RCAF, or RNZAF) training units are mentioned on a regular basis. Most of them have long and "multi-worded" titles, and rather than refer to them by these full and cumbersome terms, they are sometimes identified in the text by their acronyms. Included in the list that follows are other acronyms and words which may appear in the text, but which do not refer to units.

| | | |
|---|---|---|
| AC1 | - | Aircraftman Class 1 |
| AC2 | - | Aircraftman Class 2 |
| AFU | - | Advanced Flying Unit |
| AGS | - | Air Gunnery School |
| ANS | - | Air Navigation School |
| AOS | - | Air Observers School |
| B(A)GS | - | Bombing and (Air) Gunnery School |
| Brevet aircrew pilot | - | Single winged badge denoting an qualification other than |
| ED | - | Embarkation Depot |
| EFTS | - | Elementary Flying Training School |
| HCU | - | Heavy Conversion Unit |
| ITS | - | Initial Training School |

| | | |
|---|---|---|
| ITW | - | Initial Training Wing |
| LAC | - | Leading Aircraftman |
| ORB | - | Operational Record Book |
| OTU | - | Operational Training Unit |
| (P)AFU | - | Pilots Advanced Flying Unit |
| PRC | - | Personnel Reception Centre |
| R/T | - | Radio Telephone |

Serial Number (Aircraft) - A unique five characters given to, and appearing on, each and every RAF aircraft. Initially made up of one letter plus four digits (e.g. A1234) it became two letters plus three digits (e.g. AA123) when Z9999 was reached. Some letters have been omitted as they could lead to confusion (e.g. I, Q, and U) whilst those serial numbers starting with K or F as the first of the two letter component denote aircraft built in the USA and/or Canada. Not all possible permutations have been used.

| | | |
|---|---|---|
| SFTS | - | Service Flying Training School |
| WO | - | Warrant Officer |

Unit Code - Two character, usually alphabetic, code allocated to every RAF flying unit during World War II. During the later stages of the war some of these codes became alpha-numeric. This code was applied to all the aircraft of a unit together with a third letter which identified individual aircraft within that unit e.g. AB-C. This code was not unique, as it could be used over and over again as aircraft were replaced or lost.

# WHAT?

"Oh! I have slipped the surly bonds of Earth

And danced the skies on laughter-silvered wings;

Sunward I've climbed, and joined the tumbling mirth

Of sun-split clouds - and done a hundred things

You have not dreamed of - wheeled and soared and swung

High in the sunlit silence.  Hov'ring there,

I've chased the shouting wind along, and flung

My eager craft through footless halls of air.

Up, up the long delirious burning blue

I've topped the wind-swept heights with easy grace,

Where never lark, or even eagle flew.

And, while with silent, lifting mind I've trod

The high untrespassed sanctity of space,

Put out my hand, and touched the face of God."


Pilot Officer John Gillespie Magee

These words were written by a 19 year old American airman serving in the
Royal Canadian Air Force, whilst based in Britain.  They probably
encapsulate precisely the thoughts, which prompted many young men to
volunteer to become airmen during World War II, and nearly all those

young men who now lie beneath the Border's sod, and whose last resting place is a military grave, were airmen.

They came from all over the British Commonwealth; and once the war had started from those countries which Germany overran and occupied as the conflict progressed. To the vast majority of them joining the RAF (or RCAF, RNZAF or RAAF) was an opportunity for adventure and the exciting chance to fly, which they would never have had but for the existence of hostilities. Any altruistic ideas about defeating an "evil" or indeed any acknowledgement that they may be placing themselves in grave danger were secondary, but nevertheless important thoughts, as they began their training to become fledgling aircrew.

And dangerous it certainly was. Even the process of flying had an element of danger in it, for the aircraft of those times were not nearly as reliable as those of today, and their behaviour in given conditions not nearly so predictable.

An aircrew training plan had been put into place extremely early in the war. The agreement settling the terms of the plan was signed on 17th December 1939 by the four participating nations, Britain, Canada, Australia and New Zealand. The objective of the British Commonwealth Air Training Plan (BCATP) was to train large numbers of aircrew, and whilst doing so to make use of the under-utilised open spaces of the three Dominion countries. This was so that the demands of flying training did not conflict with those of operational flying in the increasingly congested air space over Britain. By far the largest contributor to the plan in terms of airfields, equipment and staff was Canada, although all the signatory nations provided some element of training. Indeed some basic flying training was carried out in South Africa and Southern Rhodesia (now Zimbabwe). In addition some airmen received their basic training in the USA, although this was not under the auspices of the BCATP. By the end of hostilities the BCATP had trained more than 131,000 aircrew and cost the Canadian Government $Can900,000,000. Britain's contribution to this expense was that, under the terms of the agreement, it would purchase a larger proportion of its wheat than hitherto from Canada.

The training of all aircrew was a lengthy and complex process. For those destined to be pilots it began at an Elementary Flying Training School (EFTS). Here they were taught the basic rudiments of flying, and this involved little more than the ability to get the aircraft airborne, and

13

then get it back on the ground safely again. Basic manoeuvres such as turns, climbs, and descents would also be learnt during this phase of their training. Having completed this stage of their instruction, and incidentally gained the much coveted wings, they went on to an Advanced Flying Unit (AFU). Here they would fly more complex and powerful aircraft, although not combat types. It was during the later stages of this period of training that a pupil pilot's aptitude would be assessed and a decision made as to what types of aircraft he would fly operationally. If he were adjudged to be a prospective bomber, or transport aircraft pilot, rather than a fighter pilot, he would be introduced to flying simple multi-engined (usually twin) aircraft at this stage.

During this phase of training accidents were comparatively few. This was in part due to the fact that the aircraft used were relatively slow, docile and low powered, and that an instructor was usually on hand to correct any handling errors the pupils made.

On completion of this part of their training those pilots destined to become fighter pilots went to an Operational Training Unit (OTU). These units were equipped with operational combat type aircraft of the same models, which served with operational squadrons. Unfortunately, many of the aircraft at OTU's were "hand-me-downs" from operational squadrons, having been replaced there by newer aircraft possibly of an improved mark, and as such they tended to be fairly worn and hence unreliable. This was only one factor which made this stage of a wartime pilot's training possibly the most dangerous one, perhaps even more dangerous than operational flying, and accidents were a common occurrence. Another factor that contributed to the danger was that these inexperienced pilots were suddenly asked to fly a very high powered, single-seater aircraft. It was akin to changing from driving a standard family saloon car to driving a Formula One Grand Prix car.

Approximately sixty per cent (60%) of the young airmen laid to rest in the Borders died whilst undertaking this stage of their training.

Those going on to become bomber, transport or night fighter pilots would also progress to an OTU. It was here that they would meet up with, and form their crews. The navigators, flight engineers, wireless operators and air gunners all came to the OTU's from their respective training establishments, where the majority of the syllabus was ground based, although some flying training had to be carried out.

Once these crews had gelled as a team, and become proficient in handling the aircraft at the OTU, they were sent to a Heavy Conversion Unit (HCU). At OTU's all training was carried out using twin-engined obsolescent bomber aircraft. By the third year of the war the majority of the main bomber force was equipped with four- engined aircraft, and the task of the HCU was to train the fledgling crews to operate these much larger and complex aircraft. Naturally, those crews training to operate night fighters or twin engined light or medium bombers did not need to undertake this last stage of training.

And once having completed their training course and been posted to an operational squadron, aircrew, especially fighter pilots and night fighter crews spent much of their flying time in practice in order to maintain and hone their skills. The need to push the performance of these aircraft to their limits, together with a degree of youthful exuberance, made it inevitable that accidents occurred.

At the fighter OTU's and operational day fighter squadrons, practice "dog fights" and general combat manoeuvring were common forms of training. The closing speed of these fighters when in these type of manoeuvres was very high, and as a result it was very easy for the less experienced and perhaps overconfident fledgling fighter pilots to misjudge distances between aircraft. It was unavoidable in these circumstances that mid air collisions occurred, and indeed they were an all too frequent happening.

Another major contributor to the flying accidents in the Borders was the large areas of high ground located relatively close to the airfields. When these hills were shrouded in cloud and hill fog, they could not be seen, and any aircraft not aware of its exact position, either horizontally or vertically was in grave danger of colliding with them. Unfortunately, due to navigational techniques which were far from exact, a number of aircraft did in fact suffer this fate, and became victims of the hills. Tragically aircraft accidents by their very nature tend to be destructive and dramatic. They are unforgiving, and there were very rarely survivors.

The ultimate fate of the victims of these accidents was never altogether certain. For those who had next-of-kin living in the UK, the RAF (strictly speaking the Air Ministry) offered two options.

The first of these was that the body would be transported to the home of the next-of-kin, and they, the family that is, would make the funeral arrangements, although the Air Ministry would pay for the funeral expenses. These burials were most often in the churchyard of the victim's home town. A RAF officer(s) would attend the funeral as a representative of the unit with which the unfortunate airman had been serving at the time of his death. The headstone for the grave was supplied by the Commonwealth War Graves Commission, and the grave would be maintained in perpetuity by that organisation.

Alternatively, if for some reason the family did not want to accept the first option, then the RAF would organise the funeral and the casualty would be buried in one of those cemeteries, normally attached to the Parish Church closest to an airfield. The location of the cemetery chosen for the burial, however, did not seem to be governed by any consistent policy, at least during the early years of the war. This has resulted in some haphazard locations, and not least a few anomalies, which at first sight do not appear to have an explanation. As before, all the expenses involved were borne by Government agencies.

Naturally, the option of sending the body to the family was not available for those airmen from either Commonwealth or occupied countries, the distances involved and the uncertainties of war-time overseas transport making it unviable. These airmen were buried in those cemeteries close to RAF airfields, although the same comments about inconsistency and anomalies also hold true for this group of airmen.

The burials of Polish airmen who died in the Borders are a good example of this inconsistency. In September 1941 the Polish crew of a Bolton Paul Defiant, which crashed near Edlingham, were buried at Chevington, whilst in January 1943 five Polish crew of a Wellington, which crashed on Dunmoor Hill, were buried at a dedicated Polish serviceman's cemetery at Newark. Neither of these aircraft was stationed locally. Only four months later however, the Polish pilot of a Blackburn Botha, which crashed while on a training flight for Air Gunners, was buried in the cemetery attached to Morpeth Parish Church. It is true that the aircraft was based at RAF Morpeth, but it crashed only a few miles from where the Wellington had done so. So why then was the Polish pilot of an Avro Anson based at RAF Ouston, which had a mid-air collision in October 1944 with another aircraft of the same type, but based at RAF Morpeth, buried at Chevington?

Similar, but sometimes even odder inconsistencies occurred with the burial of Commonwealth airmen, who died in the area, whether serving with a unit based at one of the local RAF stations or not. By the summer of 1943 however, dedicated cemeteries for Commonwealth

16

servicemen in general, and airmen in particular had been established. These were located at various centres throughout the UK, each serving a particular area. For north-east England this cemetery was established within the existing cemetery at Stonefall, on the outskirts of Harrogate.

The existence of these cemeteries did not prevent further anomalies from happening

# WHERE?

"Hills gently sink and valleys gently fill

The flattened fields grow ludicrously small;

Slowly they pass beneath and slower still

until they hardly seem to move at all

Then suddenly they disappear from sight,

hidden by fleeting wisps of faded white."


Jeffery Day


The four cemeteries, which contain the graves of the airmen featured in this guide, are all located in the North Northumberland/Border area. They are all close to the sites of World War II RAF airfields, only one of which is still operational. In fact very little remains to remind us that they ever existed.

RAF Acklington was opened in 1938, a result of the mid-1930's RAF expansion plan. This plan was a response to the increasingly belligerent attitude being adopted by Nazi Germany. During World War II it became a base for both day and night fighters providing the mainstay for the air defence of the north east of England. It was ideally placed for this task, being situated only a few miles from the east coast, about 7 miles south south east of Alnwick, and approximately 20 miles north of the Tyneside/Wearside conurbation. Throughout the course of the war many squadrons were based at RAF Acklington, some only staying for a few days, whilst others remained for much longer periods.

Amongst the more notable squadrons based at Acklington was 43, the Fighting Cocks, who were stationed here twice. Their first visit started in November 1939 and ended in February 1940, when they moved to Wick. Just before they left, two of its pilots, Flight Lieutenant C B Hill and Sergeant F Carey shot down a He III into the sea off Coquet Island. The second visit lasted from October 1941 until June 1942. It was during this period that the squadron suffered a number of tragic flying accidents in which, unfortunately, there were some fatalities.

**RAF 'Eagles' on top of the World, at operations site, RAF Milfield. (Photo: the author).**

Several Commonwealth airmen were involved in these incidents, and they were interred at Chevington cemetery. However, they were not the first, nor by any means the last airmen to be laid to rest there, for this cemetery had already been used by RAF Acklington on previous occasions. Indeed the first burial had taken place in October 1939, when 152 Squadron was being reformed at Acklington, and Sergeant T Mycroft was killed, when the Hawker Hart he was ferrying from RAF Turnhouse for use by the newly formed squadron, crashed in the Cheviot Hills in poor weather. Sergeant Mycroft was serving with the RAFVR, and his family lived in South East London. The headstone of his grave is unusual, in that it is not of the usual

CWGC pattern. Other airmen, including some from the Luftwaffe, had also been buried here, when their aircraft, although not based at Acklington, had crashed in the local area. At this time Acklington was the only RAF establishment in the area.

In May 1941 Acklington received its first night fighter squadron, this being 141 Squadron flying Defiants. This was quickly followed by the formation of 406 Squadron, a wholly Canadian unit, just over a week later. This squadron was flying Bristol Beaufighter MKII's. The Beaufighter, although an excellent aircraft and a superb gun platform at normal operational flying speeds, was a tricky aircraft to handle at low speeds having a tendency to "swing" violently. Unfortunately the Mark II, which was powered by Rolls-Royce Merlin engines, and the only Mark to be so, seemed to suffer more from this trait than its Bristol Hercules powered stablemates. The ultimate effect of this, of course, was yet further accidents, and unfortunately there were fatalities for this squadron, too, before it left Acklington in January 1942. Once again Commonwealth airmen were involved, and they were also interred at Chevington.Squadrons came and went right up until the closing stages of the war, and flying accidents continued to occur, but only two more Commonwealth or occupied country airmen lost their lives, and were subsequently buried at Chevington as a result.

57 OTU was a dedicated Spitfire training unit. Originally formed in June 1940 as 7 OTU, but renumbered as 57 OTU in December 1940, it was first based at Hawarden in North Wales. Whilst based there future fighter aces such as "Johnnie" Johnson and "Screwball" Beurling gained their first experience of flying a Spitfire with 57 OTU. However, Hawarden airfield was attached to Vickers-Armstrong's Broughton factory, which was producing Wellington bombers, and was also home to 48 MU, whose function it was to prepare those aircraft for operational use. As a result the airfield became too busy for comfort, and in November 1942 57 OTU was transferred to the barely completed airfield at Eshott, a few miles north of Morpeth, and bordering the Great North Road. Facilities at Eshott were basic, as it had never been intended that the airfield would be anything other than temporary. 57 OTU would be the sole user of this airfield until the end of hostilities.

An airfield was also opened at Boulmer at around the same time, and this became a satellite for Eshott with many of 57 OTU's training flights being carried out from there. In a much truncated form it is, today, the only one of the airfields mentioned in this guide to remain operational with the RAF.

OTU's were well known for their high accident rates, and 57 OTU was certainly no exception. It had suffered a number of fatalities whilst based at Hawarden, but after its transfer to Eshott these seemed to become more frequent, with an average of two fatalities per month during 1943 and 1944. Many of these were as a result of mid-air collisions (MACs) and 57 OTU did seem to have experienced a higher than normal quota of this type of accident. Although all were tragic, one is worthy of special note here. Although both pilots were strangers to the shores of the UK, neither of them, both having lost their lives, are buried locally and therefore would not have justified an inclusion in this guide.

On 12th April 1944, a Republic P47D Thunderbolt, serial no 42-25530 of the 366 Fighter Squadron of the USAAF flown by 1st Lt. Anthony L Serapiglia was taking part, together with three other aircraft of the USAAF, in simulated strafing attacks on vehicle convoys on the A1 road. All four aircraft were attached to the Fighter Leaders School (FLS) at RAF Milfield. Their pilots may have been unaware of the existence of RAF Eshott, and as they made their third pass on the convoy, they unwittingly entered the circuit of RAF Eshott, but unfortunately in the wrong direction. Several Spitfires were already in the circuit and one, serial number R6762, flown by Sgt Kai Arter Knagenhjelm, a Norwegian serving with the RAFVR, had just received permission to land, when it was

**Memorial Window to the Fallen Airmen of RAF Milfield. (Photo: the Author).**

21

in collision with the Thunderbolt flown by Lt. Serapiglia. Both aircraft went out of control and crashed to the ground close to Eshott airfield, neither pilot having had time to abandon their respective aircraft. Lt. Serapiglia was buried initially at the American Military Cemetery at Maddingley near Cambridge, but his remains were returned to the USA soon after the war for burial by his family. Sgt Knagenhjelm was cremated at Honor Oak, North London.

Many of 57 OTU's Commonwealth and overseas casualties whilst based at Eshott are buried at Chevington, and their stories are related in this guide.

Mention has already been made of RAF Milfield. Superficially its history would seem to suggest that it was just another of those multitude of training airfields at which little of any great significance appeared to have happened. But nothing could be further from the truth. Opened in August 1942 it first became home of 59 OTU, a Hawker Hurricane training unit, which transferred in from RAF Crosby-on-Eden in Cumbria. Like 57 OTU it had already suffered an unfortunate share of fatal accidents before reaching Northumberland, and these continued to occur at Milfield. Another airfield had been built at Brunton, to the north-east of Alnwick, and this became a satellite of Milfield. Its facilities were very basic, and although training was carried out at Brunton, mostly to relieve the congested air space at Milfield, no aircraft or personnel were based there on a permanent basis.

Early in 1943 the structure of the training scheme at Milfield began to alter, the first indication of the importance to the allied air campaign over the D-day beaches, that it was to attain. During March 1943 an operational squadron was based at Milfield, albeit for training purposes. This was 164 Squadron,

**Airmen's graves in Kirknewton Chhurchyrard.**
**(Photo: The Author).**

22

which was equipped with Hurricane IID's. These aircraft had originally been equipped with a 40mm cannon under each wing, and were intended to be "tank busters". But having just converted from the much more nimble Spitfire, 164 Squadron found these aircraft difficult to handle. The cannons were removed and replaced by launcher rails for four three inch rocket projectiles under each wing. The squadron then went on to a period of training involving attacking mock targets on the beach at Goswick, a few miles to the south of Berwick. These rocket attacks were delivered from very low altitude, and a special unit was set up at Milfield to train instructors in the skills of this form of air warfare. It had the unwieldy title of Specialised Low Attack Instructors School (SLAIS), and was officially acknowledged as being in existence in June 1943, although a former member of 164 Squadron, Ron Seward, records that he attended a SLAIS course during their stay at Milfield in March 1943.

By this time the Hurricane was being phased out as an "air-superiority" or interceptor aircraft in the United Kingdom and over Europe, this role being taken over almost exclusively by the Spitfire. The Hurricane, however, did still have other important functions to fulfil. It still continued to be used as a fighter in the Middle and Far East, and was being employed more frequently as a ground attack aircraft. It was utilized as a fighter-bomber, a rocket-projectile launcher and equipped with the two 40mm cannons mentioned previously, became a very effective "tank buster". And hence there was still a need for up and coming pilots to be trained to fly Hurricanes.

At about this time another Hawker fighter aircraft, the Typhoon, finally threw off all its developmental teething problems, and started to equip operational squadrons. Being a much larger and faster aircraft than the Hurricane, it was felt that a special conversion unit should be established in order to train pilots to fly it, especially in the ground attack role. It had already been recognised by the Air Ministry that the Typhoon, although initially designed as an interceptor, was ideally suited for this purpose. With facilities already on hand at Milfield, it was a natural progression for this Typhoon conversion unit to be stationed there. No special unit was formed, the Typhoon Conversion Course being run within the existing structure and administration of 59 OTU. The first course was held in June 1943.

By late 1943 the planning for the invasion of Europe was well advanced, and it was acknowledged that ground attacks by fighter-bombers in large numbers on enemy troop formations, would play a significant part in the forthcoming campaign. It was also recognised, however, that there would not be either the time or the facilities to train every single fighter pilot of the Allied Air Forces in the skills of low level ground attack. To overcome this problem it was decided that a training unit should be set up where senior flying personnel (i.e. those in command of wings, squadrons, and, if facilities and time allowed, flights), would train together to develop new tactics, and ways in which they could be utilised. They would then take these newly acquired tactics back to their own units and, hopefully, pass on those skills to the other members of that unit during routine training. In fact an embryonic version of such a training unit already existed. Known as the Fighter Leaders School (FLS) it had first formed in January 1943 as an offshoot of 52 OTU, and was based at RAF Chedworth in Gloucestershire. Its function was to train Flight and Squadron Commanders in fighter tactics.

The FLS moved to RAF Charmy Down (Somerset) in February 1943, and then to RAF Aston Down (Gloucestershire) in August 1943. During this time it was always associated with and operated as part of 52 OTU. Soon after moving to Aston Down, 52 OTU was disbanded, but the FLS continued to operate. Plans, as outlined previously, were already in place to transfer it to Milfield, where its activities would be expanded, and the emphasis placed on low-level ground attack rather than interception. Apart from the name the new unit would be totally different from the previous one. The choice of Milfield was logical in that it already had in place the facilities, such as target ranges, for training in low-level ground attack tactics, but more than that, it had a far drier climate than Aston Down, and would therefore lose fewer flying days to poor weather. The FLS moved into Milfield on the 31st January 1944, 59 OTU having disbanded on the 26th. The FLS brought most of its aircraft in the shape of Spitfires, from Aston Down, but also acquired the Typhoons left behind by 59 OTU. Interestingly, some of the Spitfires brought to Milfield were still recorded as serving with 52 OTU, although that unit had officially disbanded in the previous August. In fact these aircraft carried the same unit codes (see Glossary for explanation of term), as they had when serving with 52 OTU.

Just before the FLS moved to Milfield and planning for its move was being finalised, Air Chief Marshall Sir Trafford Leigh-Mallory, who was the Commander-in-Chief (CinC) of the Allied Expeditionary Air Force (AEAF), made the following statement -

"I want this course to take precedence over current operational commitments and all officers attending to enter into the spirit and urgent purpose for which it has been formed. Nothing could be more important to the success of operation "OVERLORD" than to train to meet the enemy at the outset at the top of our form. There is no doubt that his first impressions at the initial clash will have the most far reaching effect on the final issue."

The FLS remained at Milfield throughout the summer of 1944, but once the D-day invasions had taken place, then the need for training relented somewhat and activities became less frenetic. Not only RAF (or attached Dominion Air Force) pilots took part in the training courses at Milfield, but also Fleet Air Arm (FAA) pilots and pilots from the USAAF. The latter brought their own aircraft with them, but quite often all pilots attending a course would fly all types of aircraft available to that course. On the whole this apparently did not cause the problems, which it might be thought could be associated with pilots flying unfamiliar aircraft.

The FLS transferred out of Milfield on December 27th 1944, and was replaced by 56 OTU, a unit specialising in training pilots to operate Typhoon and Tempest aircraft.

There were numerous accidents at Milfield involving all the units stationed there, and many had fatal results. It was almost inevitable, given the number of Commonwealth airmen serving in the UK, that regrettably some of them were numbered among these casualties. There seemed to have been no single common cause for these accidents, but once again mid-air collisions appeared to have been fairly common. What certainly was not a factor, was the closeness of the Cheviot Hills to the airfield. Those same hills are close to the last resting place of some of the unfortunate victims of Milfield's accidents in the churchyard of St Gregory's Parish Church at Kirknewton. Some of the Commonwealth airmen, who lost their lives whilst serving at Milfield, are buried there, but it is known that others are buried elsewhere.

Several miles to the north of Milfield two more airfields had been opened in May 1942. These were Charterhall and Winfield, and they were situated in the broad valley of the River Tweed and sandwiched between the Cheviot Hills to the south and the Lammermuir Hills to the north. Winfield was a satellite of Charterhall and only one unit, 54 OTU, occupied these airfields during the period of hostilities.

In the early stages of the war Luftwaffe night bombers could strike at the UK almost with impunity. The only defence against them was anti-aircraft artillery and the employment of single engined day fighters by night. This latter option achieved very little success, because of the difficulty of locating the enemy aircraft. However, two types of aircraft had been found unsuitable as day fighters, and these two types the Bolton Paul Defiant and the Bristol Blenheim, were "relegated" to the role of nightfighters. Although having shortcomings for daytime operations, the fact that both types carried an extra crew member meant that there was an extra pair of eyes to look for the enemy aircraft in the night sky. The Blenheim, being a twin engined aircraft, also had a greater endurance, and therefore had a greater length of time to complete a successful search for its prey. It also had the capacity to carry aloft the first airborne radar interception equipment (AI). The first versions of this equipment were not only very unreliable, but difficult to operate and interpret. But by the end of 1940 a reliable and more user-friendly version had been developed, and was being fitted not only to the Blenheim, but also to the Bristol Beaufighter, a new twin engined fighter just entering service. The Beaufighter, although developed through the Bristol Beaufort from the Blenheim, was much faster and more manoeuvrable than the Blenheim. By March 1941 five out of the six night fighter squadrons of RAF's Fighter Command were operating AI equipped Beaufighters, and successes against enemy night bombers increased significantly. These RAF night fighters worked in conjunction with radar stations on the ground known as Ground Controlled Interception (GCI) stations, and because of the complexities of the aircraft and its radar equipment together with the techniques of co-operation with the GCI stations, a specialist night fighter OTU was established. This was 54 OTU and was initially based at RAF Church Fenton in Yorkshire. It was transferred to Charterhall/Winfield in early May 1942.

As well as the pilots having to learn to fly the Beaufighter, the radar operators (officially known as Radio Observers) not only had to learn how to use the AI equipment, but also the technique of being guided to their targets by a GCI station.

There were many accidents at Charterhall/Winfield; in fact so many that the airfields were awarded the epithet of "Slaughter Hall" by those who served there, as many of these accidents had fatal results. Once again it was almost inevitable that Commonwealth airmen were involved. Although there was no common cause for these accidents the Beaufighter's notorious "swing" on take-off and at low speed was probably a contributory factor to many of the accidents. This swing was particularly pronounced in the Rolls-Royce Merlin engined Mark II Beaufighter, with which together with some ageing Blenheims 54 OTU was equipped during its first two years at Charterhall. However, mid-air collisions (MACs) did not seem to have been such a frequent happening as at Eshott and Milfield. However, the previously mentioned "swing" on take-off did account for a large number of ground collisions, although these very rarely resulted in fatalities.

Most of the Commonwealth airmen who lost their lives whilst serving at Charterhall are buried at Fogo Church cemetery. In addition one other Commonwealth airman, although not serving at Charterhall, is buried at Fogo, his aircraft having crashed in the area.

Other airfields in Southern Scotland and Northumberland contributed to the aircraft operating over the Border Area. North of the Border RAF East Fortune, near Dunbar, was re-opened in 1940, having been an airship base during World War I. It was first used as a means of easing the congestion in aircraft movements at nearby RAF Drem, a fighter airfield. It soon became surplus to requirements for this purpose, and in June 1941 became home to 60 OTU, a Bolton Paul Defiant training unit. The Defiant, however, was nearing the end of its useful operational life, and the need for training crews to fly it ceased to exist. So the OTU started to train Beaufighter crews for the strike role within Coastal Command, and eventually changed its identity to 132 OTU. Both of these units suffered fatal accidents over the Border Hills, and one Polish crew is buried at Chevington.

Further south, in Northumberland were the airfields at Tranwell (known as RAF Morpeth), and Ouston. RAF Morpeth was the home of 4 Air Gunnery School. It too suffered fatal accidents, but none of the casualties are buried in the four cemeteries covered by this guide. One of its aircraft, however, was in a mid-air collision with an aircraft from one of the training units, 62 OTU, based at RAF Ouston. One of the crew, a Polish airman of this second aircraft is, however, buried at Chevington.

Tranwell is a few miles west of Morpeth, whilst Ouston is a few miles south of Stamfordham, and approximately 12 miles west of Newcastle-upon-Tyne city centre.

However, a number of the airmen buried in the Borders area were crew members of aircraft, which although they crashed in the area, were not stationed at any of the local airfields. These aircraft started their fateful last flights from airfields situated in other parts of Great Britain, and occasionally as far away as East Anglia. Some of these planes came to grief on the high ground in the west of the area. Other aircraft crashed on these hills, whose Commonwealth or exiled crew members, if fatally injured, were not buried in the area. Because of this their stories are not included in this guide. (See Appendix 1.)

<blockquote>
"Nor should we grieve or yearn<br>
For what is past.<br>
This place, designed for war has served its turn<br>
Let nature now take back its own.<br>
The ravages of age and time can not decay<br>
The greater work.<br>
These artefacts of steel and concrete pass away;<br>
The deeds remain."
</blockquote>

# WHO?

"From afar they battle for our ancient island_
Soaring, and pouncing, masters of the skies.
They are heard in the night by lands betrayed and captive
And a throbbing of hope to their thunder throb replies.
To dare incredible things, from the ends of the ocean
They are coming and coming, over the perilous seas
How shall we hail them?  Truly there are no words
And no song worthy of these.

from "Airmen from Overseas" - Lawrence Binyon


That these young men from distant shores flew over the Borders and subsequently lost their lives has already been acknowledged and is beyond dispute.

But what train of events had brought each man to the area, and what were the circumstances of their untimely and tragic deaths.

This guide will give, in most cases, a brief description of each mans service history; sometimes with some detail of their life before entering military service, and concluding with details of the accident in which they lost their lives.

Unfortunately the amount of detail in each story is not uniform. This is due to various factors, which include the material recorded in archives not being consistent, the access to some archives still being restricted, and whether or not contact could be made with family, friends or even service colleagues of the deceased airmen.

The stories of the airmen are told in chronological order of the dates on which they lost their lives.

## PILOT OFFICER W. ROBERTS, RNZAF AND

## PILOT OFFICER K. BROOKE-TAYLOR, RNZAF 07/04/1940

By early April 1940 the war had been in progress for seven months, and apart from isolated incidents like the naval action at the mouth of the River Plate in South America, the British Armed Forces had seen very little action. In fact so little had been happening that the period had earned itself the nickname of "The Phoney War".

Bomber Command of the Royal Air Force was, however, in action against Germany from the day war was declared. True, most of the sorties involved only small numbers of aircraft, and those over land were either reconnaissance flights or were to drop propaganda leaflets. The only targets attacked with bombs were major units of the German Navy whilst in port. But during the last two months of 1939 the British authorities became increasingly worried by the number of mines being laid around the coast of Britain by German seaplanes. These seaplanes were operating from bases in the Friesian Islands, and in an attempt to prevent this from happening, aircraft from various squadrons of Bomber Command were sent out to patrol above the bases of these mine laying seaplanes, in the hope that the mere presence of an enemy aircraft would discourage them from taking off.

The first of these sorties had taken place in December 1939, and they continued into mid-January 1940. These first patrols were carried out by Armstrong Whitworth Whitleys of 4 Group, Bomber Command. When the patrols re-started in mid-February the responsibility for carrying them out passed to the Squadrons operating Handley-Page Hampdens within 5 Group.

One of these Squadrons was 83 based at RAF Scampton in Lincolnshire. This airfield later achieved fame as the base from which the "Dambusters" raid departed. On the evening of Saturday 6th April 1940 one of 83 Squadron's Hampdens L4054 was prepared for a security patrol over the Friesian Islands. The operation had been given the mission serial number CES125, and the aircraft took off from Scampton at 19.20 hours.

The pilot of the aircraft was Pilot Officer Wilfred Roberts, whose home was in Remuera Auckland, New Zealand, although he had been born in Brisbane, Australia in 1914. He had been a keen and gifted sportsman, playing rugby for Auckland Grammar School 1st XV and also hockey for the same school's 1st XI. He passed the Auckland University College entrance exam and gained a hockey blue whilst a student there. In November 1936 he applied for a short service commission in the Royal Air Force, and on acceptance left New Zealand on the 14th August 1937 for the United Kingdom.

He commenced his elementary flying training at the Civil Flying School, Anstey, Warwickshire on the 27th September and completed the course there, before being posted to RAF Uxbridge on the 28th November for a short disciplinary course. On the 11th December with the rank of Acting Pilot Officer he was posted to No. 10 Flying Training School at Abingdon, where he was awarded his "wings" on the 28th April 1938. Now confirmed in his appointment to Pilot Officer, Wilfred Roberts was posted to the School of Air Navigation at RAF Manston in July 1938. After completing the short navigation course there, he joined No. 83 Bomber Squadron at RAF Scampton on the 22nd October 1938. He converted to Hampdens, and was still serving with the Squadron at the outbreak of war. He did, in fact, take part in Bomber Command's very first operation of the war on the 3rd September 1939, which was an intended attack on the German North Sea Fleet.

Pilot Officer Keith Brook-Taylor, although trained as a pilot, was acting as Observer for the mission of the 6th April 1940. The term "Observer" was used at this period of the Royal Air Force's history for the crew position which later became known as "Navigator", and it was normal procedure within the Hampden equipped squadrons of 5 Group for this position to be filled by a pilot. This was due to an acute shortage of qualified observers, and many pilots from 5 Group were sent on "crash" navigation courses. Keith Brooke-Taylor was from Wellington, New Zealand. He had matriculated from Wellington College in 1934 at the age of 15, and from then until he applied for a short service commission in the RAF in December 1937, had worked as an optical mechanic. He came to the United Kingdom in July 1938, and commenced his elementary flying training at Hatfield, Hertfordshire on the 29th August. He was posted to No. 3 Flying Training School, South Cerney, Gloucestershire on the 29th October, where he gained his "wings" on the 4th March 1939. On the 9th June he joined 185 Squadron at RAF Thornaby, and started to fly Avro Ansons and Hampdens with this unit. The squadron moved to RAF Cottesmore in Rutland, and in October he was transferred to 83 Squadron at Scampton. This Squadron had a detached flight at RAF Lossiemouth,

31

and it was from this base that Pilot Officer Brooke-Taylor had taken part as captain of a Hampden in four separate operational "sweeps" over the North Sea during February and early March. He returned to Scampton on the 19th March 1940.

The other two members of the crew were Sergeant A McNicol, Wireless Operator/Air Gunner and LAC D.W. Sharpe, also a Wireless Operator/Air Gunner.

The aircraft headed out over the North Sea. It was only heard from twice before being sighted again, this being when it tried to contact the RAF Station at Heston. Whether this was to try to establish its position or to report the progress and results of its patrol, is not recorded. But at around 04.00 hours on Sunday the 7th April, RAF Usworth reported a friendly bomber following a varied track between Acklington and Tynemouth. A little later Usworth reported the aircraft sending SOS signals, presumably by Aldis lamp, as there was no mention of radio contact having been made.

Lights were lit at both Acklington and Usworth airfields, but at 04.15 seemingly unable to work out their exact position and probably running out of fuel (by now the aircraft had been in the air for over 9 hours), three of the crew abandoned the aircraft after continuing to circle St Mary's Lighthouse, still sending SOS signals. By now the lighthouse had switched on its main beam and had rotated it to point to Acklington airfield. The aircraft had been given this information and instructed to follow the beam by signal lamp. Its only response to these Morse messages had been an acknowledgement that they had been received and understood. At 04.25 the Hampden was reported to have crashed at Old Hartley Village, a quarter of a mile north of St Mary's Lighthouse. The wreckage of the aircraft caught fire and burnt out.

The crew's parachutes were blown out over the sea. At 07.20 Scampton received a message relating the fate of the aircraft and its crew. Pilot Officer Roberts was picked up from the sea by a steamer (identity not known) and taken to the Naval Hospital at Blyth, where unfortunately he subsequently died. Some time later the bodies of Pilot Officer Brooke-Taylor and Sergeant McNicol were recovered from the sea.

Because of the strange behaviour of the aircraft before its abandonment and subsequent crash, the site was visited by a team from the Air Investigation Branch of the Air Ministry. This was on Monday the 8th April.

They found evidence of human remains among the wreckage. They also discovered that the aircraft had suffered far greater damage than would have been expected from the crash alone. They concluded that the small number of bombs which the Hampden was carrying had exploded on impact and that LAC Sharpe had been killed and his body almost totally destroyed by the blast.

The wreckage was so fragmented that it was impossible to locate a technical cause for the accident.

However, a returning Armstrong-Whitworth Whitley, which had passed through the patrol area of the Hampden, reported seeing an aircraft being 'coned' in a searchlight beam and receiving hits from AA fire and tracer, whilst in that area. No other aircraft returning from a mission that night reported being fired on, so it was deduced that L4054 must have been the aircraft attacked.

The crash investigators concluded that the aircraft had been disabled by this attack. The hydraulic system had probably been damaged, with the result that the undercarriage could not be lowered, or the bomb-bay doors opened in order to jettison the bombs.

As'LAC Sharpe did not abandon the aircraft it was thought he might have been injured or killed by enemy fire. Given these circumstances, the captain of the Hampden, Pilot Officer Roberts, decided to circle around a landmark until it became light and the fuel was used up. In this way he would have a better chance of either making a safe 'wheels-up' crash landing or abandoning the aircraft in a known area.

The first choice would have given LAC Sharpe a greater chance of survival, assuming he had only been injured.

In fact, it is thought that the aircraft ran out of fuel before dawn, as witnesses on the ground reported that one of its engines stopped just before the three parachutes of the crew were seen.

The chances of this theory being correct are further strengthened by the fact that LAC Sharpe was the wireless operator and his being severely injured or killed would account for the lack of any radio signals being received from the aircraft since the transmissions to RAF Heston at around 21.50 hours. It would possibly also account for the complete absence of signal lamp messages from the aircraft in response to those sent to it. LAC Sharpe would be the only member of the crew literate on Morse code.

This account is slightly at odds with other published accounts

("Bomber Command Losses of the Second World War, Vol I" by W.R. Chorley, and "The Hampden File" by Harry Moyle), which state that the aircraft crashed into the sea, and that all three airmen were already dead when recovered from the sea. What certainly is true is that L4054 was the first Hampden to be abandoned whilst on operations, and was to remain the only abandonment of a Hampden in which all of those who did so perished after leaving the aircraft. These members of the crew had been remarkably unlucky, for if they had delayed their abandonment for another few minutes, it is very probable that they would have landed on dry land rather than the sea. The North Sea would have had a temperature of only 2-3°C at that time of year, and it is very likely that these airmen suffered from the effects of hypothermia.

The incident is not mentioned at all in the RAF Acklington ORB, and neither is the burial at Chevington of Pilot Officers Roberts and Brooke-Taylor.

It therefore seems rather odd that they were buried at Chevington, as RAF Usworth and its nearest cemetery would have been closer to the site of the incident, and it was RAF Usworth whilst not only recording the events in their own ORB, who also informed RAF Scampton of the eventual outcome.

The date of their funeral is not recorded.


## FLIGHT SERGEANT W.H. TREWIN, RCAF, AND

## SERGEANT R.L. WARD, RCAF, (USA) 03/09/1941

The Battle of Britain had been fought and won, and the RAF had been engaged in its long and costly bombing offensive against Germany for more than a year, before the next Commonwealth airmen were buried in a Borders cemetery.

The War Cabinet was always acutely aware of the threat posed to the convoys of merchant ships crossing the North Atlantic by the large battleships and battle-cruisers of the German Navy. The convoys were Britain's lifeline and attempts to reduce the threat were made by either trying to blockade these capital ships in port or destroying them by bombing.

One such ship was the "Prinz Eugen". Early in September 1941 she lay in Brest Harbour. ideally positioned to slip out into the Atlantic and decimate the British convoys. It was decided to try to destroy her as she lay in port, and on Wednesday 3rd September a force of 140 bombers was dispatched in an attempt to do just that. Included in this force was an Armstrong-Whitworth Whitley V, Z6869 of 58 Squadron coded GE-T. (See Glossary). The aircraft took off from its base, RAF Linton-on Ouse, at 19.21 hours, but at 20.30 because of worsening weather conditions the aircraft was recalled. The weather at RAF Linton-on-Ouse had also deteriorated, and GE-T was ordered to land at Acklington rather than its own base.

The crew consisted of Pilot and Captain, Pilot Officer A.A. Law, Second Pilot, Flight Sergeant Wallace Howard Trewin of the Royal Canadian Air Force, Observer, Sergeant Robert Lawrence Ward also of the RCAF, Wireless Operator, Sgt C.O. Steggall and Air Gunner, Pilot Officer E.D. Comber-Higgs.

Flight Sergeant Trewin came from Toronto. However Sergeant "Larry" Ward, although officially described as serving in the RCAF, was an American from Virginia Beach, Virginia. He was a married man, and like many other young American men, had wanted to get involved in the war, but because the USA was neutral at the time, he could not do so. The RCAF made it quite clear that they would accept volunteers from the USA, even setting up recruiting offices in a few of the major US cities. And this was the route by which Sergeant Ward had become a member of aircrew with 58 Squadron.

Pilot Officer Law must have been coming near to the end of his operational tour, because it is known that he flew an operational mission as early as the 17th April 1941. This was a mission to Berlin, when the aircraft he was captain of, Whitely V T4266, GE-O, was hit by anti-aircraft fire which wrecked the port engine. As a result the aircraft

35

had to be ditched in the North Sea. On the 20th April Pilot Officer Law and the rest of his crew, which included Sergeant Steggall, were spotted in their dinghy by an overflying aircraft, and sometime later that day were rescued by an Air-Sea Rescue Launch.

On the night of 6th August 1941, Pilot Officer Law was again accompanied by Sergeant Steggall, when their aircraft, a Whitley V, Z6835 GE-Q, overshot the runway at Linton-on-Ouse whilst attempting to land on return from a mission to Frankfurt. The aircraft crashed into a hangar. Apparently there were no injuries.

But on the night of the 3rd September Pilot Officer Law, Sergeant Steggall, and the two members of the RCAF were not to be so fortunate. On the approach to land at Acklington the Whitley undershot the runway, crashed into a field at Turnbull Farm, and burst into flames. The crash occurred at 23.45 hours. Only Pilot Officer Comber-Higgs survived the crash, although he was badly injured.

The two members of the RCAF, Flight Sergeant Trewin and Sergeant Ward together with Sergeant Steggall were buried on Monday 8th September 1941 at Chevington. Their headstones show their date of death as the 4th September 1941. This is probably because although the aircraft crashed at 23.45 on the 3rd September, the resulting fire prevented death certificates being issued until the early hours of the 4th September.


## PILOT OFFICER W. BLASINSKI AND SERGEANT S. SADAWA - 05/09/1941

Only two days were to elapse after the crash of Whitley Z6869, before airmen from RAF Acklington were once again called upon to attend the scene of a fatal crash.

At 10.50 on Friday 5th September 1941 Bolton Paul Defiant N1679, of 60 OTU was on a training flight from RAF East Fortune, when it struck high ground whilst attempting to fly below low cloud. A RAF accident report records that the crash occurred at Edlington Hill, Edlingham. But no location of that name is known to exist. However, there is a location known as Eglingham Hill near the village of Eglingham, and furthermore it is known that an aircraft crashed there in the early autumn of either 1940 or 1941. Unfortunately the 60 OTU operational records show the accident as having occurred at Edlingham

Hill, Edlingham and although not shown on modern OS maps, part of the high ground to the south of the Alnwick to Rothbury road near Corby Crags, used to be known by that name. Given the confusion between the two RAF accident records (Air Ministry Form 1180 and unit ORB), which is not aided by the almost illegible handwriting in which one of them is written, and the extreme closeness of Eglingham and Edlingham, both in spelling and geographically, it is impossible to be precise about the exact location of this accident. However, the identity of the aircraft which crashed at Eglingham Hill is almost certain to be Spitfire L1094 of 610 Squadron, which crashed in early November 1940. This fact effectively rules out this crash site as that of Defiant N1679, leaving only the Edlingham Hill site as most probably its final resting place. This supposition is supported by some vague local recall of an aircraft, type unknown, crashing in that area.

The two occupants of the aircraft, Pilot Officer Wladyslaw Blasinski and Sergeant Stanislaw Sadawa, were killed instantly. There is some speculation as to the roles of these two Polish airmen, but all surviving RAF records show Pilot Officer Blasinski to have been the pilot of the aircraft and Sergeant Sadawa the air gunner. Polish Air Force records reveal that Pilot Officer Blasinski had undergone flying training whilst in the UK. He had attended a grading course at 1 (Polish) FTS, Hucknall from May to June 1941. Sergeant Sadawa, on the other hand is not recorded as having received any flying training, his only instruction being in air gunnery at 4 BGS, West Freugh. This would seem to confirm the roles of the two airmen.

Pilot Officer Blasinski was 24 years of age and had served as an officer cadet at Dzebhin in Poland. Like the 29 year old Sergeant Sadawa he had arrived in Britain via Romania and France.

60 OTU had been stationed at East Fortune since June 1941. Pilot Officer Blasinski and Sergeant Sadawa were included in No. 3 Training Course, which had commenced on 7th July 1941, and was due to conclude on 8th September 1941, and therefore at the time of the accident would have been becoming a reasonably competent crew. Although the weather at East Fortune was clear when the aircraft took off, it was described as being "low cloud and bad visibility" in North

Northumberland, and a subsequent report on the accident concedes that given the existence of these weather conditions, authorisation for the flight should not have been given.

Pilot Officer Blasinski and Sergeant Sadawa were both buried in Chevington cemetery on Tuesday 9th September 1941.

The investigation into the causes of the accident was carried out by Flight Lieutenant Petrie, who arrived at RAF Acklington on 10th September.

## PILOT OFFICER R.S. AUSTIN, RNZAF AND

## FLIGHT SERGEANT W. STUART, RCAF 06/09/1941

The two Polish airmen were not alone in having a RAF funeral at Chevington cemetery on the 9th September. They were joined by Pilot Officer Richard Scott Austin of the Royal New Zealand Air Force and Flight Sergeant William Stuart of the Royal Canadian Air Force.

Hardly had RAF Acklington had time to recover from the crashes of Whitley Z6869 and Defiant N1679, when yet another Whitley, Z6932, this time of 10 Squadron, crashed in the area and became the station's responsibility. This happened on Saturday 6th September, and once again poor weather was a contributory cause of the accident.

Flight Sergeant Stuart, the captain of Z6932, was a native of Victoria on Vancouver Island. He had joined the RCAF on the 19th July 1940 at Calgary. Initially posted to 1 Manning Depot (an initial training unit) at Toronto, he started his flying training on the 7th October 1940 at 5 EFTS stationed at Lethbridge. He was transferred to 3 SFTS at Calgary on 29th November, where he gained his "wings" and was promoted to Sergeant on the 15th February 1941. His next posting was to Debert, Nova Scotia on the 12th March, but it is unlikely that he undertook any flying training at 7 OTU, which was based there, as on the 25th March he left for the UK, arriving on the 17th April. On the 21st April he was posted to 19 OTU, a Whitley training unit at RAF Kinloss, and having completed his course there, transferred to 10 Squadron at RAF Leeming on the 8th July. It is not clear whether he formed part of a regular crew at Kinloss, who then all transferred to 10 Squadron at the same time, but that is likely to have been the case as Sergeant Stuart was the captain of a crew, which remained constant for at least five operational missions.

However, on the night of the 31st August/1st September 1941 the regular 2nd pilot of that crew, Sergeant Rochford, was replaced by Pilot Officer Richard Scott Austin, when they flew Whitley Z6478 on a mission to Essen.

Richard Austin was born at Paluatua, New Zealand on the 29th September 1919. Having attended the High School there, he became a law clerk employed by a local firm of Solicitors. Like most young New Zealanders he was a keen sportsman, playing Rugby for his School 1st XV and later taking up both golf and swimming.

He enlisted in the RNZAF at the Initial Training Wing, Levin on the 28th September 1940. He started his flying training at 3 EFTS, Harewood on the 27th October, and moved on to 2 SFTS Woodbourne (also known as Blenheim) on 26th December. Gaining his "wings" on the 10th February 1941, he was then granted a commission with the rank of Pilot Officer on the 22nd March. He arrived at 3 PRC, Bournemouth on the 3$^{rd}$ June, and was posted to 10 OTU, another Whitley training unit at RAF Abingdon on the 7th June. Having completed his course he was then posted to 10 Squadron at Leeming on the 30th August, and the next day flew on his first, and, as it turned out, his last operational mission.

Sergeant Stuart by this time was a "veteran" of a previous 9 missions, 5 of these being flown as 2nd Pilot with other crews. His first operational mission as captain was to Ostende on the night of 18th/19th August in Whitley T4234. The next four missions, including that of the 31st August, when the 2nd Pilot's position was filled by Pilot Officer Austin, were flown in Z6478.

On the evening of Saturday 6th September 1941 10 Squadron were due to provide aircraft for an attack on the German industrial town of

Huls. Early that afternoon Whitley Z6932, coded ZA-Y, took off from Leeming for an air test prior to taking part in this operation. However, the weather was very poor with persistent rain and low cloud, and the aircraft became lost. This is not entirely surprising, as there was no navigator on board, the crew consisting of Pilot and Captain, Sergeant Stuart, 2nd Pilot, Pilot Officer Austin, Wireless Operator, Sergeant P.W. Bryant and Air Gunner, Sergeant R. Whitlock. In order to establish his position Sergeant Stuart descended through cloud with the intention of landing. He did so on the incomplete Brunton airfield, which was still under construction at the time. On taking off the aircraft hit some barrels, which caused it to veer off course and strike a steam roller. It did, however, still manage to become airborne, but only just, and the aircraft was probably not under proper control when it had to avoid some high tension power cables, and in so doing stalled and crashed. Sergeant Stuart, Pilot Officer Austin, and Sergeant Bryant were all killed instantly, but Sergeant Robert Whitlock survived, although badly injured, and was admitted to the Royal Victoria Infirmary in Newcastle. The site of the crash was very close to Brunton airfield, and may have even been within its perimeter, because all three airmen who died are described as having done so at "Brunton Aerodrome, Northumberland" in casualty records.

There has always been some confusion as to where and when this crash actually occurred, and the above narrative is at odds with some previously published accounts. Two of these ("Bomber Command Losses of WWII, Vol II 1941, W.R. Chorley, and "Northumberland Aviation Diary", Derek Walton) state that the aircraft crashed at Acklington, having collided with high tension power cables, one account stating that this happened on the following day, Sunday 7th September. This is probably because both Sergeant Stuart's and Pilot Officer Austin's CWGC headstones erroneously show their dates of death as the 7th September.

However, both the 10 Squadron and RAF Leeming ORBs record the incident, including the names of the casualties, as happening on the 6th September, and in fact record the time of having received the report from Acklington as 16.15 hours. The Acklington ORB does not mention the incident at all, apart from the burial of Sergeant Stuart and Pilot Officer

Austin on Tuesday 9th September, and since Brunton airfield was yet to be opened it did not have an ORB at that time.

The official accident report on Air Ministry Form 1180 (and probably extracted from the results of a Court of Enquiry) definitely gives the place of crash as Bruton (misspelt), near Chadhill (also miss-spelt). This has led the incident to be recorded in the "The Whitley File" (an Air Britain publication) as having occurred at Bruton, Somerset! The fact that casualty records show the place where those casualties occurred to have been "Brunton Aerodrome", make the possibility of there being any other site for the crash to be almost impossible.

The Official War Diary of the RNZAF in WWII concurs with the present narrative, when it records Pilot Officer Austin's death. It also records that he had completed 235 hours of flying in total.


## FLYING OFFICER HUGH JOHN FINDLAY, RCAF AND

## FLIGHT SERGEANT EDWIN KARL VICKERS, RCA 14/09/1941

When Bristol Beaufighter II R2473 crashed on its final approach to land at Acklington on Sunday 14th September 1941, killing both of its crew, the officers and men of the station must have started to wonder if a curse had been put on their establishment. For this was the fourth fatal accident in less than a fortnight, and eleven young airmen had lost their lives. This time however, the aircraft was not from a distant station but was from 406 Squadron, RCAF, based at Acklington, and the loss was probably even more keenly felt.

This squadron had been formed at Acklington in May 1941. It operated Beaufighter IIs in the night fighter role. Flight Sergeant Vickers had joined the squadron on the 23rd June 1941. A native of Toronto, he had enlisted in the RCAF there on the 15th April 1940. Following initial training he had been instructed as an air gunner at Jarvis, gaining his Wireless Operators/Air Gunners (WAG) brevet on the 25th November 1940. He arrived in the United Kingdom from the embarkation pool at

Halifax on the 2nd March 1941. He was posted to 15 OTU at Harwell on the 15th March 1941, possibly with the intention of him becoming a member of a bomber crew as 15 OTU operated Wellingtons, and was a training unit within Bomber Command. Plans must have changed however, for on the 4th April 1941 he was posted to No.1 Signal School, Cranwell, where he stayed until his transfer to 406 Squadron.

Flying Officer Findlay was born in 1913 in Castleton Place, Ontario. He studied law at McGill University from 1932 to 1936, graduating with a BA degree. Further studies followed at the Osgood Hall Law School, Toronto, and he became a LLb, barrister and a Member of the Ontario Bar in 1939.

He enlisted in the RCAF on the 9th October 1939 at Ottawa. Details of his training are not well documented, but it is known that he gained his pilot's wings on the 29th April 1940, and that he did so while serving with The Central Flying School at Trenton, Ontario. He like Flight Sergeant Vickers was also posted into the squadron on the 23rd June. Although a single man when he joined the RCAF, by the time he came to the United Kingdom he was married. His wife, Jessie Carroll Findlay, lived at Westmount, Quebec. Flight Sergeant Vickers was also married, his wife Mary, living in Toronto.

It would seem that by the date of the accident, Flying Officer Findlay and Sergeant Vickers were not considered "combat ready", and had not been added to the list of operational crews. They therefore had not taken part in any operational duties.

On the night of Sunday 14th September 1941 Flying Officer Findlay and Flight Sergeant Vickers climbed into Beaufighter II R2473, and took off on a GCI (Ground Controlled Interception) Exercise. Although Beaufighters had their own airborne radar equipment to locate their target aircraft, it was only capable of detection over a short range, and so they were guided to their targets by instructions given to them by operators of very powerful radar equipment with a much longer range, located on the ground. Once the Beaufighter was in the proximity of the target aircraft, it could then use its own radar to locate the target precisely. It was a complex operation, and needed total understanding and teamwork between not only each of the crew members, but also between the crew and the operators on the ground. The object of the flight that night was to practice that technique.

The exercise complete, the aircraft returned to Acklington. It made a normal circuit and approach, but suddenly dived into the ground approximately 2 miles south west of the airfield. The aircraft simply lost flying speed and stalled. No apparent reason for this was ever established, but it was not thought that an obstruction on the leeward end (i.e. downwind) of the Acklington, runway, which had been marked with red "glims" was a contributing factor. The accident occurred at 23.57 hours on the 14th, but is not recorded in Acklington's records until 00.23 hours on the 15th September. The location of the crash is given as Brunton Park, but no place of that name can be found on a modern Ordnance Survey map.

The two airmen were buried at Chevington on the 17th September 1941.


## SERGEANT JOHN ALLAN RYERSON TURNER, RCAF
## 12/10/1941

Sergeant Turner was still to arrive at Acklington, when the last of the previous accidents had occurred. But within two weeks of his arrival, he too had perished, and had been laid to rest in Chevington cemetery.

Sergeant Turner enlisted in the RCAF in Ottawa on the 10th October 1940. He must have been a rapid learner, because by the 15th July 1941 he had progressed through 10 EFTS at Mount Hope, Hamilton, and 2 SFTS at Uplands, Ottawa, and gained his pilot's wings. On the 4th August 1941 as a member of the RAF Trainees Pool, he embarked at "Y" Depot, Halifax on his passage to the United Kingdom. Arriving in Britain on the 16th August 1941, he was quickly posted to 55 OTU at RAF Ouston on the 21st August 1941. Although officially transferred to 43 Squadron at Acklington on the 30th September 1941, the squadron records show Sergeant Turner as "posted in" on the 7th October 1941.

43

On Sunday 12th October 1941 Sergeant Turner took off in Hurricane Z2807 to practice dogfights with Pilot Officer Hutchison in Hurricane Z3270. One series of practice attacks had been completed, and then a second series of attacks started at around 16.50 hours. Pilot Officer Hutchison was to be the target for this second round of attacks, but unfortunately Sergeant Turner misjudged the timing of his attack, and overran Pilot Officer Hutchison's line of flight. The propeller of Pilot Officer Hutchison's aircraft struck and cut off the tail of Sergeant Turner's aircraft, which went into a spin and crashed near Alnwick. Pilot Officer Hutchison managed to crash land his damaged aircraft near Embleton, only suffering slight injuries as a result of the accident.

Sergeant Turner, however, did not survive the crash of his aircraft.

It is not known when Sergeant Turner was buried, but he had only served five days with 43 Squadron, when he lost his life.

## PILOT OFFICER HERBERT BASIL WOOLER, RAFVR
### 08/01/1942

The spate of accidents which had plagued Acklington during September and early October came to an end, and for a couple of months there were no more Commonwealth or foreign casualties.

This spell of good fortune was broken on the evening of Thursday 8th January1942, when Beaufighter II T3037 of 406 Squadron RCAF crashed at Stobswood Colliery, Widdrington, killing both of its crew. The pilot was Pilot Officer H.B. Wooler, whose home was at the Halfway Tree, St Andrew, Jamaica, although he had been born at Clerks Town on the same island. His Radar Operator/Observer was Sergeant T Williams of Llandeilo, Carmarthenshire.

The aircraft had taken off at 21.05 on a routine patrol, but at 21.15 was observed to emerge from cloud, appeared to stall and then spun into the ground.

Little is known of Pilot Officer Wooler's previous history in the RAF, apart from that he enlisted on the 2nd September 1940. None of the standard documentation, which would normally have been raised as a result of a flying accident, can be brought to light. These documents would have yielded more information concerning Pilot Officer Wooler, especially in respect of the extent of his flying experience. It is known that he was posted into the Squadron on the 28th November 1941, and that previous to that date had served at 54 OTU at RAF Church Fenton, where presumably he had received his "conversion" training.

Pilot Officer Wooler was buried at Chevington cemetery at 14.30 on Tuesday 13th January 1942.

The funeral was attended by Mr S.S. Wooler, an uncle, and also Mr N.S. Shaw, a family friend from Ilkley, Yorkshire.

Sergeant Williams was buried in his home town on the same day as his pilot.

## SERGEANT LAURENCE WARREN HUNT, RNZAF AND

## SERGEANT THOMAS WALTER IRVING, RNZAF 15/01/1942

The night of Thursday 15th January 1942 proved to be an expensive one for RAF Bomber Command. For of 96 aircraft despatched to bomb Hamburg, only 52 claimed to have bombed the target. But more importantly 12 aircraft were lost, when they crashed in the United Kingdom on their return, due to the appalling weather conditions. Four of these aircraft crashed on high ground in the North of England.

One of these four aircraft was Vickers Wellington Z1078 coded JN-L (see Glossary) of 150 Squadron, which crashed on the northern slope of the Cheviot in an area known as West Hill.

The aircraft had taken off from RAF Snaith its home base, at 17.25 on the same day. Included in the crew that night were Sergeant L.W. Hunt RNZAF, who served as second pilot and Sergeant T.W. Irving RNZAF, who was the Navigator/Observer.

**Sgt. L. W. Hunt RNZAF (Photo: Mrs L. Rodgers)**

Sergeant Hunt was the son of a dairy farming family from Albany, part of Auckland's North Shore area on New Zealand's North Island. Immediately after the outbreak of war he volunteered for the RNZAF, and after a concentrated correspondence course in Maths, Geometry and Trigonometry, entered the Basic Training Course at Wararoa, Levin, in December 1940. He was posted to No. 4 EFTS at Whenuapai, Auckland in February 1941, where he received his initial flying training in Tiger Moths. On the 29th April 1941 he was transferred to the BCATP, and arrived at No. 12 SFTS Brandon, Manitoba, Canada on the 25th May 1941. He received training on Cessna Crane twin engine aircraft, and gained his "wings" on the 30th July 1941. He was then transferred to the United Kingdom via "Y" Depot, Halifax, Nova Scotia, arriving at No. 3 Personnel Reception Centre, Bournemouth on the 15th September 1941. From there he was transferred to 23 OTU at RAF

Pershore for the final stages of his training and incorporation into a crew. 23 OTU operated Wellington aircraft, and towards the end of their training period there, under training crews of this unit took part in leaflet dropping raids ("Nickeling") over occupied France.

Sergeant Irving came from the Dunedin area of New Zealand. After leaving school he was employed as a blacksmith with New Zealand

**Graduation & Presenting of Observers' Wings No 6 Prince Albert, Canada. T.W. Irving back row, 4th from right. (Photo: Mrs N. Johnson).**

Railways. He was accepted as an under training air observer by the RNZAF on the 5th January 1940. This had been his second attempt to volunteer. He entered the Ground Training School, Levin on the 22nd December 1940, and on the 27th February 1941 set out for Canada under the BCATP. His first posting in March 1941 was to No. 6 Air Observers School, Prince Albert, Saskatchewan, followed in June 1941 by a move to No. 3 Bombing and Gunnery School, MacDonald, Manitoba. He completed his training at No. 1 Air Navigation School, Rivers, where he was awarded his Air Observer's "wing", and promoted to Sergeant on the 22nd July 1941. Like Sergeant Hunt he came to Britain via "Y" Depot, Halifax, Nova Scotia and arrived at 3 PRC, Bournemouth in September 1941. After an initial posting to 11 OTU at RAF Bassingbourne on the 14th October 1941, he was transferred to 23 OTU only a few days later.

Along with Sergeant Hunt, Sergeant Irving joined a crew captained by Pilot Officer B.A. MacDonald, a 21 year old Canadian from New Waterford, Nova Scotia. Completing the crew were Sergeant W.H. Allworth, a Wireless Operator/Air Gunner, Sergeant F.G. Maple and Sergeant C.F. Glover who were both Air Gunners. During the last phases of their training at 23 OTU in keeping with other advanced crews, they took part in leaflet dropping ("Nickeling") missions over Occupied France.

In early December the crew were transferred to 150 Squadron based at RAF Snaith in East Yorkshire. Before the night of the 15th January the crew had taken part in bombing raids on three previous occasions. These were to Boulogne on the 27th December 1941 and to Brest on the 6th and 9th January 1942, and all had utilised Wellington I Z1078, JN-L.

Sgt. T.W. Irving RNZAF, on final leave 1941. (Photo: Mrs N. Johnson).

The raid to Hamburg had met with little opposition. But on their return to the United Kingdom all of the aircraft encountered atrocious weather conditions including snowstorms. Z1078 must have lost track of its position due to these weather conditions, and at 23.55 was seen to crash into West Hill by a young shepherd, Arch

Guthrie. He was returning from a dance in Wooler to his home at Southernknowe, when he witnessed the crash and the subsequent fire.

Despite the fact that a blizzard was raging and regardless of his own safety, Arch Guthrie started to make his way up to the site of the crash, calling in en-route at the house at Southernknowe. From there he was accompanied by James Goodfellow, the head shepherd. On arrival at the crash site they found a survivor sheltering behind a rock. They led this man to safety in the farmhouse at Dunsdale, which was closer to the site of the crash than Southernknowe, although the route still lay over some steep, rugged and difficult terrain. Having made the survivor comfortable, John Dagg, the shepherd at Dunsdale, returned to the crash site with James Goodfellow, whilst Arch Guthrie went off to Hethpool, some 4½ miles to the north to alert the authorities. On reaching the crash site, having used John Dagg's horse, the two shepherds discovered two more survivors, who were only superficially injured, an airman who was very badly injured, and two airmen who were already dead.

By this time the fire in the wreckage was extinguished, and it was only the smell of burnt aircraft fabric, which led the shepherds to the crash site in conditions of almost zero visibility.

The critically injured airman, Sergeant Irving, was carried back to the house at Dunsdale. Given the weather conditions, and that it was night time plus the difficulty of the terrain which had to be crossed, this journey must have been very difficult and physically demanding. Despite all their efforts Sergeant Irving succumbed to the combined effects of his injuries and hypothermia before medical assistance arrived.

The following morning when daylight broke, the bodies of Sergeant Hunt and Sergeant Maple were recovered from the hillside, and together with Sergeant Irving's were taken to RAF Acklington. All three men were buried with full military honours at Chevington on Monday 19th January 1942 at 11.00.

The bleak hillsides of the Cheviots had taken their toll, and two more of New Zealand's sons were now at rest below the turf of Northumberland.

But such were the fortunes of war in the air and military flying, that only one of the three survivors of the crash was alive, when peace came to the world again in 1945. This was Sergeant Glover, who then led a quiet, unassuming life before passing away in 1993, aged 75.

P/O B.A. MacDonald had been promoted to Flight Lieutenant by the time he, too, lost his life in a flying accident on the 11th August 1943, whilst flying a Mosquito, an aircraft type he was converting to with 1655 MTU based at RAF Marham in Norfolk.

Sergeant W.H. Allworth also died as the result of a flying accident. This was on the 10th October 1942. When piloting a Wellington of 150 Squadron on a training flight, he lost control of the aircraft whilst attempting to land in gusting cross winds at RAF Elsham Wolds. The Wellington crashed near the runway, and Sergeant Allworth suffered injuries from which he subsequently died.

### SERGEANT FRANK ERNEST HAINES, RCAF 26/03/1942

By March 1942 the Bolton Paul Defiant was almost at the end of its operational life as a fighter. In fact within two months no aircraft of the type remained in an active combat role. It had been a huge disappointment. Its unique and innovative feature, the revolving gun turret, reduced all aspects of the aircraft's performance and made it extremely vulnerable to attack by opposing single seater fighters. It was removed from use as a day fighter and utilised as a night fighter, a role in which the extra pair of eyes of the gunner gave it a slight edge over a single seater aircraft. It had a modicum of success in this role and the RAF persevered with its use, though with the benefit of hindsight they should probably have abandoned their efforts to utilise it, and redirected both the manufacturing capacity and training of crews into newer and more capable aircraft.

On the evening of Thursday 26th March 1942, 410 Squadron RCAF only had a few days left operating their Defiants. Their main base was at Drem, but they had detached flights at RAF Acklington and RAF Ouston. At 20.45 hours Defiant N3364 took off from Drem with Sergeant Haines as pilot and Flight Sergeant J.A.G. Pelletier as gunner.

A native of the Province of New Brunswick Sergeant Haines had enlisted in the RCAF at Moncton, on the 9th November 1940. His initial flying training took place at 3 EFTS, Victousville, but on 22$^{nd}$ June 1941 he was transferred to 9 SFTS at Summerside, and gained his "wings" there on the 1st September 1941. Passing through 'Y' Depot, Halifax on the 3rd September 1941 he arrived at 3 PRC, Bournemouth on the 28th September. He was transferred to 56 OTU at RAF Sutton Bridge on the 8th October, and stayed there until posted to 410 Squadron on the 19th February 1942.

Enemy raiders had been detected over the North Sea on the evening of 26th March, and the crew of N3364 had been ordered to wait above base for the raiders to come inland before attempting an interception. At 22.30 however, the aircraft was over the Farne Islands and the pilot was overheard on the R/T to tell the gunner to bale out, as there had been a massive instrument failure. The rear gunner did as instructed. At midnight Control reported that the aircraft had crashed. At 02.00 hours it was confirmed that the aircraft had definitely crashed, and that the pilot had been killed. The location of the crash is described as Haredean, 6 miles north-west of Morpeth, and also as Beacon Hill, Longhorsely.

Sergeant Haines was buried at Chevington on Monday 30th March 1942 at 11.00 hours. Pilot Officer D.B. Freeman, RCAF, Pilot, and Flight Sergeant E. Torpy, RCAF, Air Gunner, attended the funeral as representatives of the Squadron. Sergeant Haines was just 19 years old.


## FLIGHT SERGEANT H.J. HELBOCK, RCAF (USA) 05/04/42

Even before WWII had commenced, the effects of 'G' force on the pilots of the extremely fast and manoeuvrable new monoplane fighters were known and accepted. These forces, caused by the centrifuge effect of tightly turning aircraft and also their rapid accelerations and decelerations, prevented blood flowing back to the pilot's brain. If this condition persisted for too long, the pilot would lose consciousness. This process was known as "blacking out". As soon as the aircraft resumed straight and level flight and the 'G' forces were removed, the pilot's blood flow would return to normal, and he would regain consciousness. Unfortunately, during the intervening period of "blackout" he may have lost control of the aircraft, and if the aircraft then went into a spin or dive the 'G' forces instead of decreasing would be increasing, resulting in the pilot not regaining consciousness. He would then be unable to regain control of the aircraft, and a crash would be almost inevitable. During combat such "blackouts" were obviously a decided disadvantage, it being far more preferable to remain in control of one's own aircraft and also be totally aware of what your opponent was doing. Perversely, the manoeuvres carried out during combat were the most violent of all, and therefore more likely to produce "blackouts".

In 1938 a Canadian doctor, Wilbur Franks, had noted the effects of 'G' and had studied the physiology of the body's reaction, which caused these "blackouts". With funds donated by a wealthy Canadian businessman, Harry McLean, Dr Franks constructed a centrifuge. This machine could mimic the 'G' forces developed in violent manoeuvres by aircraft, and with its help he designed a flying suit of non-stretch fabric, which contained water bladders. During tight turns producing high 'G' forces these bladders became pressurised and in turn pressurised parts of the pilot's body, restricting the flow of blood away from his brain. This suit became known as a "Franks Suit". It was first tested in an aircraft, a Finch, in 1939, when Dr Franks himself became the guinea pig. The trial was a great success, and further development using a Spitfire as the test aircraft ensued. Dr Franks, who by this time had joined the RCAF and become a Wing Commander, brought the suit to Britain to be tested at Farnborough, and also at the Air Fighting Development Unit, Duxford. Eventually, by early 1942 the suit was considered to be sufficiently developed to be issued, on a very limited trial basis, to operational pilots. One of the Squadrons chosen for these trials was 43 Squadron based at Acklington.

Flight Sergeant Harley Joseph Helbock was considered to be a pilot of well above average ability. He had been posted to 43 Squadron on the 3rd December 1941.

A native of Clay, New York, USA Flight Sergeant Helbock had enlisted in the RCAF at Kingston, Ontario on 28th October 1940. After passing through the various initial training establishments where the rudiments of military life, discipline and drill were learnt, he started his flying training at 7 EFTS on 17th March 1941. He was transferred to 1 SFTS at Camp Borden on 17th May 1941, and was awarded his "wings" on 30th July 1941. He then proceeded along the now familiar route to Great Britain passing through "Y" Depot, Halifax on 19th August 1941, and arriving at 3 PRC, Bournemouth on 8th September 1941. He was posted to 56 OTU at.Sutton Bridge on the 16th September, and after completing the course there, he was posted to 43 Squadron.

On Sunday 5th April 1942 Hurricane Z2983 took off from Acklington with Flight Sergeant Helbock at the controls. He was wearing a "Franks Suit". The time was 11.55 hours. At 12.30 the aircraft crashed at South Side Farm, Lucker, killing Flight Sergeant Helbock. There was no evidence that the aircraft had suffered any technical failure. Perhaps the purpose of the flight had been to test the effectiveness of the "Franks Suit". Had Flight Sergeant Helbock performed some manoeuvres, which the "suit" had proved incapable of preventing him from suffering the subsequent "blackout", and then lost control of the aircraft? Conjecture, surely, but if the "suit" were to be tested thoroughly, then the manoeuvres would have to go to the "edge".

The "Franks Suit" was considered to be capable of giving Allied Fighter pilots a considerable advantage over their Luftwaffe opponents. As such it was deemed to be highly secret, and although some Fleet Air Arm pilots used it in action for the first time during Operation "Torch" (the invasion of North Africa) in November 1942, its existence was not disclosed until December 1944.

The 'G' suits which modern supersonic jet fighter pilots wear, are based on the original "Franks Suit", and perhaps it should be remembered that without sacrifices, such as that which Flight Sergeant Helbock made in testing the equipment, then their lives might not be so secure today.

Harley Joseph Helbock was 22 years old, when he lost his life. Only two weeks before this he had been recommended to be commissioned.

He is buried at Chevington, but the date of his funeral is not known.

## FLIGHT SERGEANT A.J. REED, RCAF 17/04/42

Less than two weeks were to pass before 43 Squadron lost another of its North American pilots.

Flight Sergeant Alexander John Reed, a native of Turtleford, Saskatchewan, had in fact enlisted in the RCAF during the same week as Flight Sergeant Helbock. By a series of coincidences each one's progress through his training periods mirrored that of the other. However, Flight Sergeant Reed's flying training commenced with 17 EFTS at Stanley, Nova Scotia. This was on 16th March 1941, one day before Flight Sergeant Helbock commenced his training. On 26th May 1941 Flight Sergeant Reed at that time an LAC, was transferred to 9 SFTS at Summerside. He gained his "wings" on 10th August 1941, at which time he was also recommended for a commission, although not granted one. Passing through 'Y' Depot, Halifax at the end of August 1941 he arrived at 3PRC, Bournemouth on 29th September. He was posted to 59 OTU based at RAF Crosby-on-Eden on 20th October for his conversion course to Hurricanes. This OTU was later transferred in August 1942 to RAF Milfield in Northumberland. He was posted to 43 Squadron based at Acklington on 17th December 1941.

By early April 1942 Flight Sergeant Reed had accumulated a total of 185 hours of flying time, of which 89 hours had been spent flying Hurricanes. On Friday 17th April 1942 he strapped himself in Hurricane IIC Z3068, and at 16.45 took off on a low flying Army co-operation exercise. This exercise had been given the code name "Oatmeal".By 17.10 Flight Sergeant Reed and the rest of his section were near Whittingham. The section leader was keen to impress and flew at ever lower altitude. Flight Sergeant Reed then made an error of judgement by

54

trying to fly lower than his section leader. The Hurricanes were equipped with cine-camera guns, so that the results of their practice attacks could be assessed.

Flight Sergeant Reed must have been giving these too much of his attention, and in so doing he failed to notice the high tension power cables of the Dunston-Edinburgh grid system, a feature he had been warned about. The Hurricane struck the cables and crashed into the side of the road, which in present times runs along the eastern edge of Thrunton Woods, where it completely disintegrated. One eyewitness of the event, Mr Bert Miller, who ran a sawmill at Whittingham Station, saw the aircraft making mock attacks on an army truck convoy travelling on the main Wooler to Morpeth road. The aircraft was flying in a westerly direction and appeared to fly through the cables, but then crashed. Willy Armstrong a young teenager, had been working in one of the meadows at his father's farm, Thrunton Redhouse. He became aware of an aircraft approaching, and then heard the nearby high tension electricity cables give a loud "twang". He looked up and saw that one of the arms on the nearby pylon had twisted around. At the same moment he also saw an aircraft obviously out of control, which then hit the road with considerable force and disintegrated.

Some time later it was rumoured that the cause of the crash may have been the late afternoon sun dazzling Flight Sergeant Reed, but that cannot be confirmed.

Flight Sergeant Reed was killed instantly. He had only recently been promoted to Flight Sergeant, and was described as "keen, but sensible".

He, too, is buried at Chevington, but once again the date of his funeral is not recorded.

## FLIGHT LIEUTENANT W.D.W. HILTON, RCAF 23/07/1942

By July 1942 54 OTU had only been operating from Charterhall and Winfield for two and a half months. It had moved into airfields far from complete, and the difficulties of trying to run a busy training programme whilst coping with putting the finishing touches to the airfields meant that some routine activities were not afforded the usual amount of attention. One of these was the compilation of the unit's Operational Record Book. For the first few months of 54 OTU's tenure of Charterhall/Winfield, the ORB contains little precise detail, so Flight Lieutenant William Deveraux Woodruff Hilton's death on the 23rd July, as a result of a crash in Beaufighter R2440, only gets a very brief mention.

He was alone in the aircraft when it crashed on the rising ground at Rules Main Farm, just to the northeast of Duns adjoining the main road to Grantshouse. It is known that the weather was very poor and visibility limited. It is not clear whether Flight Lieutenant Hilton was a student or an instructor at 54 OTU, but given his rank the latter is more likely. There is also the possibility that he may have completed a "tour" of duty flying another type of aircraft, and had been posted to 54 OTU to convert to flying Beaufighters.

The crash happened on a Thursday and is described in police records as occurring next to Hawthorn Park, the Duns cemetery.

On Saturday 25th July Flight Lieutenant Hilton was buried in that same cemetery, only a short distance from where he lost his life.

## SERGEANT T.A. RUTHERFORD, RAAF 14/08/1942

Despite the fact that Thomas Allan Rutherford served in the Royal Australian Air Force, he was born in the Borders. Ironically, fate decreed that he would also die in the Borders.

Thomas Rutherford was born in Brampton, Cumberland on the 3rd August 1922. It is not known when his family emigrated to Australia, but he was certainly there by 1932 as the Dean of Perth, when standing as Thomas's referee for his application to join the RAAF in August 1940, stated that he had known Thomas for over 8 years. He had attended Perth Boys' School from 1936 to 1938 and Perth Modern School from 1939 to 1940, and had attained a good success rate in his Junior Matriculation Exams. When he applied to join the Air Force in August 1940, having only just turned eighteen years of age, he was described as a student having no employment. His official enlistment into the RAAF was on the $3^{rd}$ February 1941, and he went directly from his home town of Nedlands to 5 ITS at Pearce, Western Australia. Like most of the raw recruits described in this guide, his first requirement was to learn the rules of military service. He had enlisted as aircrew, and on the 3rd April he commenced his flying training at 9 EFTS based at Cunderdin, Western Australia. His rate of learning must have been good, because on the 2nd June he was transferred to 4 SFTS at Geraldton, Western Australia, where he was awarded his "wings" on the 24th July. On enlistment he held the rank of AC2, being promoted to LAC on his posting to 9 EFTS, and to Sergeant on the 19th September, having completed his course at 4 SFTS. Further advanced training now beckoned, and he left Australia from the port of Newcastle on 17th November, having passed through 5 Embarkation Depot in Perth and 2 Embarkation Depot at Bradfield Park, New South Wales. He was bound for the UK, and arrived at 3 PRC, Bournemouth on the 17th February 1942, although the route he took is not recorded. But given that his journey took 3 months, then it is most likely that he came by way of the USA and Canada.

Later in the war stays at the PRCS could be quite lengthy, as constrictions in the "training chain" delayed candidates from entering the first stages of their operational training. But in early 1942 the BCATP was not in full swing and the training units in the UK were capable of accepting the whole flow of under-training aircrew. So Sergeant Rutherford was transferred to 14 (P)AFU at RAF Ossington within three weeks of his arrival in the UK. RAF Ossington was situated about 7 miles north west of Newark, Nottinghamshire, and 14 (P)AFU used Airspeed Oxfords for multi-engined advanced flying training.

On the 23rd June 1942 he was posted to 60 OTU based at RAF East Fortune, where he would encounter his first combat aircraft, the Bristol Beaufighter, with which the unit had recently been re-equipped. There were also a number of Blenheim and Beauforts serving with the unit, and these were used to introduce the trainee crews to higher performance aircraft. The advantage that the Blenheim and Beaufort had over the Beaufighter was that the instructor could sit alongside the trainee pilot, and could take control of the aircraft in the event of anything untoward happening.

At about this time the emphasis of 60 OTU's training programme changed from training night-fighter crews for Fighter Command to training shipping strike crews for Coastal Command. It may have been this change, which prompted Sergeant Rutherford's transfer from 60 OTU at East Fortune to 54 OTU at Charterhall on the 2nd August.

So when Sergeant Rutherford prepared to take-off from Charterhall in Blenheim BA192 during the very early hours of Monday 14th September, he already had three months experience of flying the Bristol "Twins". His Radio Navigator that night was Sergeant J.C. Kidd, but it is not known whether this was a regular arrangement. At 01.15 the aircraft struck a tree, and shortly after take-off, crashed at Pittlesheugh, near Eccles, approximately 2 miles south of the airfield. Sergeant Rutherford was killed instantly, and Sergeant Kidd suffered serious injuries from which he subsequently died. No explanation of why the aircraft was at a low enough altitude to make contact with the tree was put forward by the RAF. Two likely reasons suggest themselves. The first is the failure of one engine during or just after take-off. The Blenheim V's performance on one engine being so poor that it could not then gain altitude. Or that being a night time take-off Sergeant Rutherford would have been flying the aircraft on instruments, which in the dim light of the cockpit he may have misread.

Thomas Alan Rutherford was buried in Duns cemetery at 12 noon on Wednesday 16th September. He had returned to the Borders, and would not leave again.

**The graves of F/Lt. Hilton and Sgt. Rutherford in Duns
Cemetary.
(Photo: the Author).**

Several days later a Miss D.A. Brown of Newark received a
letter from the Air Ministry, confirming that her friend, Sergeant T.A.
Rutherford had lost his life in an aircraft accident. They expressed their
deep sympathy.#

### FLYING OFFICER J MORRIS, RCAF 24/10/1942

The Bristol Beaufighter has already featured several times in this
guide. And it would claim the lives of yet more Dominion airmen
throughout the Borders, before the war came to an end.

One such airman was Flying Officer John Morris, RCAF. Little
detail can be found of his training or enlistment in the RCAF, but by
October 1942 he was engaged in his operational training with 54 OTU
based at Charterhall.

Shortly after midnight on Saturday 24th October 1942 Flying
Officer Morris took off from Winfield, Charterhall's satellite airfield in

Beaufighter II R2313. He was alone in the aircraft, no navigator being on board.

At around 00.20 Walter Middlemass and Margaret and John Wight, who all lived at Greenwood Farm, Grantshouse, heard an aircraft flying north towards Drone Hill, despite the fact that a violent rainstorm was occurring at the time. This was followed by a thud. They went out to investigate what had happened, and discovered the wreckage of an aircraft in the Outer Birn Field. The police were informed, and a little later RAF personnel arrived at the scene.

The aircraft was R2313, and Flying Officer Morris was killed instantly. A report on the accident concluded that Flying Officer Morris probably failed to use his blind flying instruments correctly, when he encountered the rainstorm, and consequently lost control of the aircraft. There was also a slight possibility of one of the engines having failed, although this could not be confirmed. Flying Officer Morris had completed 178 hours of flying, including 29 hours flying Beaufighters, when the accident happened. Of this previous flying experience only 5 hours had been spent flying Beaufighters at night, and therefore necessitating the use of the technique of "Instrument Flying".

Flying Officer Morris is buried at Fogo Church cemetery.

### WARRANT OFFICER (1) G.H. NEATE, RCAF 06/11/1942

Warrant Officer (1) George Harry Fromelles Neate had the unfortunate distinction of being the first Commonwealth airman to become a casualty whilst serving at RAF Milfield.

He joined the RCAF on 23rd September1940 in his home town of Edmonton, Alberta. It is very likely that he already held a pilot's licence because his trade on entry to the RCAF is given as Elementary Flying Instructor. Although joining the RCAF as an Aircraftsman 2nd

Class, by the 3rd December1940 he had been promoted to Sergeant. From that day he served with 16 EFTS at Edmonton. His service record shows, rather oddly, that he was granted indefinite leave without pay from 12th December 1940. It is not recorded when this situation ceased, but on 10th September 1941 he was promoted to Flight Sergeant. During this time it is assumed that he was an instructor with 16 EFTS, and on 1st March1942 he was once again promoted, on this occasion to Warrant Officer (WO1). On the 15th August 1942 he passed through 'Y' Depot at Halifax, and arrived in Great Britain at 3 PRC Bournemouth on 2nd September 1942.

By November 1942 he was serving with 59 OTU at RAF Milfield. From available records it cannot be established whether he was there as an instructor or a pupil, but the former is more likely, as has already been stated, his RCAF records show his "trade" to have been "Elementary Flying Instructor", and he had attended a Flying Instructor's course at the Central Flying Training School at Trenton, Ontario.

On Friday 6th November W/O Neate and Flight Lieutenant P.A. Mortimer strapped themselves into Master I T8431 in preparation for a session of low flying instruction. The Master I was an advanced trainer powered by a Rolls-Royce Kestrel V-12 engine, and had acquired the reputation of being a delightful aircraft to fly with very few vices. Take off time is not recorded, although it must have been sometime in mid-afternoon, as the crash which ensued occurred at 15.45. The weather was described as poor to fair, with occasional patches of ground fog. There is some confusion as to which of the airmen was in control of the aircraft at the time of its crash. It was most likely to have been W/O Neate, as he had far fewer hours flying Masters (18) than Flight Lieutenant Mortimer (119), although both had a total of over 1000 hours of flying experience. It would therefore have been W/O Neate, who was under instruction and therefore he would have been in control of the aircraft.

The aircraft eventually arrived over Howburn, a farm to the south of Carham village and about 5 miles south west of Cornhill. The aircraft dived on a wood and then immediately climbed steeply to an altitude of about 1100 feet, causing it to stall. The pilot then tried to regain control by diving. However the initial stall had flicked the aircraft over so that it was facing rising ground. In order to avoid this rising ground, the pilot suddenly tried to pull out of the dive, an action which only exacerbated the situation by precipitating a high speed stall, and the aircraft plunged to the ground. In the resulting crash W/O Neate was killed instantly, and Flight Lieutenant Mortimer suffered very serious injuries to which he succumbed on the following day.

The report of the accident makes no mention of the weather conditions, despite the fact that the inclusion in the meteorological report for Milfield of the presence of occasional patches of ground fog, might suggest that conditions were not entirely favourable for low flying. The Inquiry into the crash must have concluded therefore, that the poor weather conditions were not a contributory factor to the crash.

Warrant Officer Neate was buried in the Churchyard of St Gregory's, Kirknewton. His age is not known, and his headstone is inscribed giving him the rank of Sergeant. He left a widow, Hazel, in Edmonton, Alberta.


## FLYING OFFICER T.J. DONOHUE, RAAF 10/11/1942

Flying Officer Thomas James Donohue enlisted in the RAAF on the 21st May 1942. He came from Tweed Heads, New South Wales. No further record of his service in the RAAF is available, but since such a short period of time elapsed from his date of enlistment, until him serving with 54 OTU at Charterhall, it is a distinct possibility that he already held a pilot's licence before joining the RAAF. An alternative to this is that he may have served in some form of Volunteer or Territorial Auxiliary Unit before joining the regular RAAF, and that he had learned to fly whilst serving with that unit.

In November 1942 54 OTU were still using Bristol Blenheims for the initial phases of training Beaufighter night-fighter crews. BA111 was a Mark V version of the Blenheim. This version was generally considered to have a poorer performance than the earlier marks, mostly due to the fact that the aircraft had become heavier, and acquired more drag inducing factors during its development, but still utilised the same engines as the original marks.

On the afternoon of Tuesday 10th November 1942 Flying Officer Donohue took off in Blenheim BA111 for a training session of Circuits and Landings (Colloq. "Circuit and Bumps"). It is known that by this time he had completed 161 hours of flying in total, of which only 3 had been on Blenheims. He must therefore have been at the very early stages of his operational training. At 14.20 the starboard engine failed. As the aircraft was in a sequence of take-offs, circuits, and landings it would have had a low airspeed, and probably because of his lack of experience Flying Officer Donohue lost control of the aircraft, allowing it to stall. It then spun into the ground at the Cottage Field, Kimmerghame Mains, about 2 miles south of Duns and close to the River Blackadder. It burst into flames, and in the subsequent inferno Flying Officer Donohue lost his life. He was 23 years old.

He became the second Commonwealth airman to be buried at Fogo Church cemetery. Before the war came to a close he would be joined by a further eight Dominion airmen.

(Footnote:- J.B. Thompson's excellent book "The Charterhall Story" records this accident as being due to the failure of the port engine, which is what the 54 OTU ORB records. Official documents listing the findings of a Court of Inquiry, state that it was the starboard engine which failed.)

## SERGEANT C.L. HUTCHESSON, RAAF 13/11/1942

At 11.05 on Friday 13th November 1942 Beaufighters R2378 and T3359 of 'C' Squadron 54 OTU took off from RAF Winfield. Both aircraft had been checked over by ground crew earlier that morning, and the necessary paperwork (Form 700) signed declaring that they were airworthy.

**Sgt. C.L. Hutchesson RAAF.**
**(Photo: National Archive of Australia).**

Sergeant Hutchesson was to fly R2378 with Sergeant H.M. Rickard-Bell as his Radio Navigator (Radar Operator), whilst T3359 was flown by Sergeant W.H. Vincent with Pilot Officer D.A. Thorpe as his Radio Navigator.

The purpose of both flights was an Airbourne Interception Exercise at 10,000 feet, in which T3359 flown by Sergeant Vincent was to be the target aircraft and R2378 flown by Sergeant Hutchesson the attacking aircraft. Both of the pilots were adjudged to be competent to carry out this exercise by their Instructor, Flight Lieutenant Pocock.

R2378 had been allotted the radio call sign ATORA 118, and similarly T3359 had been allotted ATORA 124 for the duration of the exercise.

At 13.25 R2378 made a climbing attack from below and behind T3359. Pilot Officer Thorpe watched the attacking aircraft approaching and informed his pilot, Sergeant Vincent, of its position. As Pilot Officer Thorpe finished his message Sergeant Vincent saw R2378 coming up under the starboard wing of T3359, and start to turn to port. It was impossible for Sergeant Vincent to take evasive action and his starboard propeller hit the port elevator of R2378. He momentarily lost control of T3359, and by the time he had regained control, the other aircraft had disappeared. Sergeant Vincent reported the accident by R/T at 13.26, and although his aircraft was damaged, he was able to land without further mishap.

William Renton was returning home to Kettleshiel Farm, near the village of Polwarth, when he saw the stricken R2378 plunging from the sky in a spinning spiral dive. The nose of the aircraft lifted on two occasions, and William Renton thought the pilot must be trying to correct the spin. He could see that the tail-plane of the aircraft was damaged, and assumed this to be reason for the pilot not being able to regain control. Shortly after the second check to its dive, the still spinning aircraft hit the ground. He immediately telephoned Duns Police Station to tell them of the crash, and then made straight for the crash site. The pilot had been thrown 50 yards from the wreckage, and was obviously not alive. Mr Renton respectfully covered the pilot's body with his parachute, and then went to look at the Radio Navigator, who was still in his cockpit. He was also dead, and as there was little more he could do, William Renton left the site, and waited for the authorities to arrive.

Upwards vision from the pilot's cockpit of the Beaufighter was good, so it is somewhat difficult to understand why Sergeant Hutchesson had not seen the target aircraft above him. However, he may have been taking instructions from his Radio Navigator, whose whole attention would have been on his instruments at this phase of the attack, and would not be visually aware of the target aircraft's position. Because of this need to listen carefully to his navigator's instructions, it is likely that Sergeant Hutchesson was probably flying R2378 on instruments, and had not seen how close he was to the target aircraft. He had approached Sergeant Vincent's aircraft from its blind spot, and the latter did not have time to take evasive action. The weather at the time of the accident was favourable with good visibility and only 2/10ths cloud.

Both pilots involved in the accident had approximately the same amount of flying experience. Sergeant Hutchesson had completed 326 hours in total with 20 hours of this being spent flying a Beaufighter. A

65

further 46 hours of this flying time had been accumulated on Blenheims whilst at 54 OTU.

Clarence Lenord Hutchesson was born in the small town of Horsham in the State of Victoria, Australia on the 29th November 1912. After attending Horsham High School, where he obtained a Merit Certificate, he went on to Longerening Agricultural College. For a short time after leaving College he worked in farming, then as a carpenter before settling down as a junior partner with his father's funeral director's business. On the 9th July 1931 he married Winifred O'Farrell. The couple had two children, Brian, born on 26th November 1933 and Lynette, born on the 3rd May 1936.

He enrolled in the RAAF Reserve on the 5th August 1940, and was fully enlisted on the 28th March 1941, when he was posted to 1 ITS at Somers. Having received his initial training, he was transferred to 3 EFTS at RAAF Essondon on the 20th June to commence his flying training. On 21st August he was transferred to 2 Embarkation Depot at Bradfield Park prior to leaving for Canada, where he would resume his flying training. He left Australia on the 18th September arriving in Canada on the 16th October. Continuing his flying training at 7 SFTS RCAF Macleod in Alberta, he was awarded his "wings" and promoted to Sergeant on the 16th January 1942. As with many other Commonwealth airmen trained in Canada, 'Y' Depot, Halifax became his home from the 14th February until the 14th March, when he embarked for the United Kingdom, arriving at 3 PRC Bournemouth on the 28th March. He was to stay there until the 30th June, when he was posted to 2 (P)AFU at RAF Brize Norton. Here he underwent advanced flying training on Oxford aircraft, and was a member of No. 18 Course. RAF Little Rissington and 6 (P)AFU were Sergeant Hutchesson's next port of call, arriving there on the 15th July. He was on No. 12 Course, but on the 8th August he was sent on attachment to 1517 Beam Approach Training Flight at RAF Wattisham. His posting to 6 (P)AFU came to an end on the 18th August, when he was transferred to 54 OTU at Charterhall, to begin his operational training as a night fighter pilot.

Tragically he did not complete his training, and was laid to rest at Fogo Churchyard at 14.30 on Monday 16th November 1942. Sadder still was that neither his wife nor his two young children would have seen him for at least 14 months, and did not have an opportunity to say their last farewells.

Friday the 13th had lived up to its reputation.


## SERGEANT A. McISAAC, RNZAF 28/11/1942

The grave of Sergeant McIsaac is not within the plot of airmen's graves at Chevington Cemetery, and is situated among the civilian graves of the cemetery.

He was not serving at RAF Acklington, and neither was he killed in a flying accident in the surrounding area. In fact he died as the result of a crash of a Stirling bomber, BF399, coded AA-O of 75 Squadron. This aircraft was on a training flight, and in trying to avoid a head-on collision with another Stirling of the same Squadron, stalled and then crashed into the ground at Trinity Farm, close to Oakington airfield in Cambridgeshire. Sergeant Alexander McIsaac was the mid-upper gunner of the aircraft.

Sergeant McIsaac had enlisted in the RNZAF on the 11th May 1941 at the Ground Training School, Levin. Shortly after this on 18th June 1941 he embarked for Canada under the BCATP. He was posted to No. 3 Wireless School, Winnipeg on the 5th July 1941. His training there was terminated late in 1941, and on the 9th January 1942 he was posted to the Composite Training School, Trenton, where he was re-mustered as an air-gunner. This suggests that he had failed to make the grade as a Wireless Operator, but this was not unusual, as a particularly high and difficult to achieve standard had been set for this trade. On the 28th February he was posted to No. 4 Bombing and Gunnery School, Fingal, Ontario, where he was awarded his Air Gunner's brevet on the 30th March. On the very next day he was transferred to 'Y' Depot, Halifax, but he had to wait over a month before he embarked for the UK, leaving on the 1st May. He arrived in the UK on the 12th May and was posted to the now familiar 3 PRC at Bournemouth. He attended a refresher course at No. 7 Air Gunnery School, Stormy Down in South Wales from the 15th July until the 4th August, when he was posted to 11 Operational Training Unit stationed at RAF Bassingbourne in Hertfordshire. Whilst there he became a member of a crew trained to operate Wellingtons, and on the 6th October this crew was posted to 75 Squadron.

This squadron acquired the title '75 New Zealand Squadron' due to the increasing number of New Zealand personnel serving with it. At the end of WW II the Squadron number and title were gifted in perpetuity to the RNZAF, in recognition of the service and sacrifices of the large number of New Zealanders, who had served with the Squadron.

Sergeant McIsaac flew four operational missions in Wellingtons before the Squadron started to convert to four-engined Stirling aircraft in November 1942. These missions were to Cologne on the night of 13th/14th October, Genoa on the night of 23rd/24th October, Milan on the night of 24th/25th October and Essen on the 29th October.

Alexander McIssac was born in Dargaville, Northern Wairoa on the 20th January 1918. His mother, Adelaide, was also born there, whilst his father, Allan Joseph was born in Invercargill. Hence there is no hint of a connection with a UK relation in general, nor with a north-east relation in particular, so it is something of a mystery as to why Sergeant McIssac is buried in Chevington cemetery. Two possible reasons suggest themselves. The first of these is that a number of New Zealand airmen had already been buried in Chevington cemetery. If that was the reason, however, why then was the other New Zealander, Sergeant R.H. Brodie (some records spell this name as Broady - the former is from New Zealand Defence Force records) killed in the same crash as Sergeant McIssac, not also buried at Chevington? The second reason is that it is possible he may have formed a romantic attachment (possibly becoming engaged) with a young lady serving in the WAAF, who at the time of his death was stationed at RAF Acklington.

Whatever the reasons may have been, he now lies in the heart of rural Northumberland, far from his home and kinfolk, and a constant reminder of turbulent times.

# FLIGHT SERGEANT R.D. MAYNARD, RCAF 14/01/1943

Richard Davies Maynard enlisted in the RCAF on the 30th May 1941. His home was at Unionville, Ontario, and his enlistment had taken place in Toronto. He was immediately given leave without pay, and this was no doubt done to allow the recruiting system to get all the necessary paperwork completed, and ensure that there was somewhere for AC2 Maynard to go to. He started his flying training at 1 SFTS Camp Borden on 10th August 1941. He was promoted from AC2 to LAC on 6th December 1941, the same day on which he was given his official trade of "airman pilot" by the RCAF. He gained his "wings" on the 19th June 1942 and was promoted to Sergeant on the same day. By this time he had returned to Camp Borden, having spent the period from the 7th December 1941 until the 1st March 1942 at 10 EFTS Mount Hope, Hamilton. Unusually Sergeant Maynard commenced his operational training whilst still in Canada. He was posted to 1 (Fighter) OTU at Bagotville, Quebec in early July 1942, and stayed there until 24th October 1942, when he was posted to the now familiar 'Y' Depot, Halifax, through which all Commonwealth airmen, who had been trained in Canada, seemed to pass when they were being posted to the European theatre of war.

The date of his arrival in the UK is not known, but by early January 1943 he was serving with 59 OTU at RAF Milfield, and had been promoted to Flight Sergeant.

On Thursday 14th January 1943 Flight Sergeant Maynard took off from Milfield in Hurricane P3411 for some night flying experience. Out of his total flying time of 192 hours only 13 had been carried out at night, and only 3 of that whilst flying a Hurricane. By 21.30 he had strayed from his intended area of training. He then entered a bank of cloud, which he was not expecting to encounter. It is assumed that he then panicked, and put the aircraft into a steep spiral dive. Without doubt he did this in order to establish his position as quickly as possible. The cloud base must have been low, as Flight Sergeant Maynard failed to correct the dive of the aircraft when emerging from the cloud, and the aircraft struck the ground. The aircraft is described as having crashed 2 miles north east of Acklington, which would put the crash site in an area just west of Gloster Hill and New Hall Farms near Amble.

Flight Sergeant Maynard was killed instantly, and is buried in St Gregory's Churchyard, Kirknewton. His headstone records his rank as Sergeant Pilot.

**Headstone of Flight Sergeant R.D. Maynard. (Photo: The Author).**

## SERGEANT M.A. DIXON, RCAF 04/02/1943

Sergeant Murray Allen Dixon is likely to have travelled to the UK at exactly the same time as Flight Sergeant Maynard, as he was posted to 'Y' Depot, Halifax on the same day, the 24th October 1942, and also left that facility on the same day, the 27th October. It is a very strong possibility that they even crossed the Atlantic on the same ship.

However, their training in Canada had followed entirely different paths. Sergeant Dixon had been brought up in Trenton, on the outskirts of Toronto, and it was there he enlisted in the RCAF on 10th September 1941. He was immediately granted the then normal period of leave without pay. With the rank of AC2 he was posted to the Manning Depot, Toronto on 27th October 1941, and from there to 3 Training Camp Headquarters in Montreal. He started his flying training at 5 Initial Training School, Belleville on 15th February 1942, leaving there on 11th April 1942, the day on which he was not only promoted to LAC, but also given his trade as aircrew "B". The next day he arrived at 20 EFTS Oshawa, Ontario to start his flying training in earnest. On the 21st June 1942 he was transferred to 8 SFTS, Moncton, and it was there he gained his "wings" and was promoted to Sergeant on 9th October 1942. Then he joined Sergeant Maynard at 'Y' Depot, Halifax.

Like Sergeant Maynard, Sergeant Dixon's date of arrival in the UK is not recorded, and although it is known that he was serving with 59 OTU at Milfield by early February 1943, the date of his transfer into that unit is likewise not known.

On Thursday 4th February 1943 Sergeant Dixon strapped himself into Hurricane II V6989. The time was about 10.00am, when he took off on a routine training flight. It was a clear, fine day.

Records do not make it clear whether Sergeant Dixon was carrying out this training alone or in the company of other aircraft. It is, however, most likely to have been the latter, because at 10.20 the aircraft was seen to go into a right hand spiral dive at 10,500 feet, and then continue in a vertical dive into the ground. Given the exactness of the altitude, which would have been unlikely from a ground eyewitness, then that information would most likely have come from the pilot of an aircraft flying close to that of Sergeant Dixon.

The aircraft crashed just to the north of the Till Bridge at Chillingham Newtown. The impact was on the west bank of the River Till, and such was its force that an eyewitness who passed the scene only a little time after the event, remarked that the only trace of the crash was a hole in the river bank with steam and smoke emanating from it. A guard of soldiers was already at the scene, although the crash had only happened about 30 minutes previously.

In a report on the accident it is surmised that Sergeant Dixon blacked-out in the first part of the manoeuvre, and then did not regain consciousness, and was therefore unable to take control of his aircraft again.

Sergeant Dixon is buried in St Gregory's Churchyard, Kirknewton. He was only 19 years of age when he died, and so must have been only just 18 when he enlisted.

### FLYING OFFICER R.C. BELL, RAAF 27/02/1943

57 OTU moved to RAF Eshott in November 1942. It had formed as 7 OTU at Hawarden in North Wales in June 1940, and was redesignated as 57 OTU in December 1940.

It was a dedicated Spitfire training unit, and during its stay at Hawarden had suffered its fair share of fatal accidents. Many of these were associated with the mountains and uplands of North Wales, which stretch across the whole width of Wales, only disappearing when the English border and the Cheshire plain are reached. Its move to Eshott did not reduce 57 OTU's accident rate, the only change being that comparatively fewer of them were associated with high ground. This was probably due to the fact that the Simonside and Cheviot Hills are further away from Eshott than the Clwydian and Ruabon Mountains are from Hawarden.

To Flying Officer Ronald Charles Bell went the unfortunate distinction of being the first Commonwealth victim of a 57 OTU fatal accident whilst stationed at Eshott, to be buried in a Northumberland cemetery.

Apart from the fact that he enlisted in the RAAF on the 15th August 1941, nothing is known of Flying Officer Bell's progression through his period of training. He was a resident of Bondi, New South Wales.

On Saturday 27th February 1943 Spitfire P8362, which was being flown by 20 year old Flying Officer Bell, was in a mid-air collision with Spitfire P8360, flown by Sergeant H. Myhre, a Norwegian serving in the RAFVR. The accident occurred over Eshott Home Farm, and unfortunately both pilots were killed. The operational records of 57 OTU at this period contain little detail, and as one of the standard pieces of documentation which should have been raised after the occurrence of a flying accident, does not exist either, then it is impossible to conclude any other facts, such as the time of day, concerning the accident.

Both Flying Officer Bell and Sergeant Myhre were buried at Chevington, but only Flying Officer Bell now remains there, Sergeant Myhre's body having been repatriated to Norway soon after the war.

## SERGEANT L. KOCOUREK RAFVR, (CZECH) 17/03/1943

At 1415 hours on Wednesday 17th March 1943 two more Spitfires of 57 OTU were involved in a mid-air collision. The aircraft then crashed at Brotherwick Farm , just to the west of Warkworth. The two aircraft involved were both Mark I Spitfires, X4266 and AR222. They were being flown by Pilot Officer J.B. Memoz, Free French Air Force, and Sergeant Ladislay Kocourek, a Czechoslovakian serving in the RAFVR, although from available documents it is impossible to tell which airman was flying which aircraft.

A report on the accident concludes that the pilot (unnamed) of X4266 was over confident in making cross-over manoeuvres during formation flying, and as a result of keeping a poor look out struck AR222.

Both airmen were killed in the accident.

Sergeant Kocourek still lies buried at Chevington, far from his native Czechoslovakia. He was born on 1st March 1918 in the town of Beno, and had escaped from Czechoslovakia to join the RAF on 24th July 1940.

73

## FLIGHT SERGEANT E.L. BROWN, RAAF 25/03/1943

The night of Wednesday 24th/25th March 1943 saw dramatic events take place in the skies over Northumberland and the Borders. A force of 25 Luftwaffe bombers (Ju88s and Do217s) had approached the area at low altitude over the North Sea. On making landfall they had dispersed and the alerted night fighters and anti-aircraft guns attacked some of them, whilst others fearful of being attacked, headed away from the main area of this defensive action. The end result of all this activity was that 4 German aircraft, 2 Ju88s and 2 Do217s lay smashed to pieces in the Border countryside. Not one member of their crews survived. Two of these aircraft crashed in the Cheviot Hills, one of which was erroneously claimed to have been shot down by a Beaufighter based at Acklington. In fact the aircraft, which was shot down, a Ju88, crashed at Earlston.

**Flight Sergeant E.L. Brown RAAF.**
**(Photo: National Archive of Australia).**

On the following morning, probably with excitement running high at the local RAF stations due to the previous nights events, a Spitfire IIB, P8587 took off from Eshott. The time was about 11.00, and the pilot of the aircraft was Flight Sergeant Eric Lindsay Brown, an Australian who hailed from Leongatha, Victoria. He was 24 years old, and had come to 57 OTU at Eshott by a rather more circuitous route than the previous airmen in this guide had arrived at their respective units.

74

He successfully applied for selection as aircrew in the RAAF on 26th July 1940, having previously made unsuccessful applications in January 1937, July 1937 and January 1939. He had been an above average scholar at school, and had gained passes in six subjects for his School Leaving Certificate (equivalent of GCSE). He had obtained further qualifications whilst attending, part-time, a technical college in Melbourne. During that time he was employed as a carpenter, but on the date of his application to join the RAAF he was out of work. Since leaving school he had also served in the 29/22 Batt, Fitzroy Militia, a form of "territorial army" unit. His application to join the RAAF was approved on 7th August 1940, but his date of actual enlistment was the 26th April 1941.

On that date AC2 Brown started to learn the basics of military discipline and drill at 1 Initial Training School, RAAF Somers, near Melbourne. Having completed this part of his training he was promoted to LAC, and posted to 1 Embarkation Depot at Ascot Vale on 21st June 1941. His eventual embarkation was delayed until 1st September 1941, when he left Sydney bound for Southern Rhodesia (now Zimbabwe), where he arrived on 10th November 1941. His first posting in Southern Rhodesia was to the Initial Training Wing based at Hillside, near Bulawayo. However, he was quickly moved on to start his flying training with 26 EFTS at Guinea Fowl, near Gwelo on 4th December 1941. No doubt having picked up the rudiments of flying fairly rapidly, he was transferred to 22 SFTS at Thornhill, also near Gwelo, on 2nd February 1942. It was here on 24th March that he was awarded his "wings", having been promoted to Acting Sergeant on transfer to the unit. Another move took him to 21 SFTS at Kumalo on 9th May, before being shipped out to Egypt on 1st July. He arrived in Egypt on 25th July, and was "shuffled" around between several units including 21 Personnel Transit Centre (PTC), 2 PRU and 22 PTC. His service record shows that during this time he was "on strength for disposal only", and was probably held in transit until suitable means became available to get him to the UK. This happened on 24th October, and his first posting was to 17 (P)AFU at RAF Watton on 26th January 1943. He had been promoted to Flight Sergeant on 19th December 1942.

He arrived at 57 OTU, RAF Eshott on 2nd March 1943. By this time he had been enlisted in the RAAF for nearly 2 years, and only accumulated approximately 100 hours of flying. Compare this to Flight Sergeant Reed, who had enlisted in the RCAF at approximately the same time that Flight Sergeant Brown had in the RAAF, but who had accumulated 185 hours of flying before his untimely death in April 1942, almost a year before Flight Sergeant Brown's transfer to 57 OTU.

When Flight Sergeant Brown took off from Eshott in P8587, he had a total of 110 hours of flying experience, of which 21 hours had been carried out in a Spitfire. P8587 was nearly two years old, and had served with three operational squadrons. On 14th January 1942 whilst serving with 132 Squadron at RAF Peterhead, it had overshot on landing and hit an obstacle on the ground, sustaining damage assessed as Category E, that is a write off. However, it was reprieved, repaired, and eventually re-issued to 57 OTU on 20th October 1942. By a strange coincidence it was to suffer another accident exactly a year later on the 14th January 1943, but this time only slight damage was caused, and the aircraft was returned to use on 5th February, having been checked over by Vickers-Armstrong engineers at their works in Oxford.

The object of the flight on the 25th March was an air firing exercise. By 11.30 it seems that Flight Sergeant Brown had strayed from his intended track. Although the weather had been clear at Eshott at the time of his take off, the conditions over North Northumberland were far from satisfactory, being 10/10ths cloud down to quite a low cloud base.

Bob Jackson was the shepherd at Goldscleugh, the small farm steading at the head of the Langdon Beck, a tributary of the College Burn in the Cheviot Hills. At around 11.30 on that fateful Thursday, he heard an aircraft approaching . Then there was a thud, followed by silence. Bob decided he should go to look to ascertain what had happened. In a short space of time he came across the wreckage of the aircraft on the ridge of Bellyside Hill overlooking Dunsdale Farm. The crashing aircraft had killed at least one Blackface ewe, and the ensuing blaze had triggered explosions of ammunition, and set the surrounding heather on fire. Bob immediately saw that the pilot was beyond assistance, and made his way down to Dunsdale to report the incident. The aircraft he had found was Spitfire P8587 with its unfortunate pilot Flight Sergeant Brown.

In a short report on the accident it is surmised that Flight Sergeant Brown may have disregarded some of his instructions, become lost in the low cloud and because of the lack of direction finding equipment at Eshott, been unable to pinpoint his exact position.

Eric Lindsay Brown was buried at Chevington cemetery on Monday 29th March 1943 at 15.00 hours. Poignantly, he had asked that in the event of him becoming a casualty, then not only should his parents be informed, but also a Miss Winifred Laurie of Raulton, Bulawayo, Southern Rhodesia. There was to be yet another young woman with a grieving, broken heart.

**Headstone of Flight Sergeant E.L. Brown. (Photo: the Author).**

## SERGEANT V. SINDELAR, RAFVR (CZECH) 19/04/1943

By 1943 the Royal Air Force had several squadrons manned totally by Czechoslovakian personnel. To replace the almost inevitable losses, and also to replace aircrew,who had completed their operational "tours", it was essential that further Czechoslovakians were trained to operational flying status. Vaclav Sindelar was just such a man.

He had joined the RAF on 25th July1940, no doubt having arrived in the UK after fleeing the Nazi tyranny, which had overrun his homeland. He was born on 21st September 1918, and was a native of the town of Elzen.

By April 1943 Sergeant Sindelar was serving with 57 OTU at Eshott. He must have been nearing the end of his course, because by Monday the 19th April 1943 he had flown 48 hours in a Spitfire out of a total of 162 hours of flying time.

At 10.35 hours on the 19th April he took off from Boulmer in Spitfire IIA P7352 in company with four other Spitfires. Sergeant Sindelar was flying No. 4. The purpose of the flight was a formation height climb. When the formation reached 11,000 feet, No. 1 instructed the pupil pilots, including Sergeant Sindelar, to check their oxygen systems. At 11.20 hours when the aircraft had reached 23,000 feet, Sergeant Sindelar's aircraft was seen to break formation and go into a steep dive. The aircraft started to break up, and this may have been due to Sergeant Sindelar attempting to make a recovery. The aircraft crashed with a huge impact about 300 metres south of Rock Hall. Sergeant Sindelar could not possibly have survived such a crash, and died instantly.

It was suggested that the most likely cause of the accident was Sergeant Sindelar "blacking-out" due to oxygen starvation. It was concluded that the reason for this was that he had coupled his oxygen mask to the economizer outlet, instead of the direct oxygen line from the regulator, and to compound the error, had failed to connect the economizer to the supply at all.

Flying Officer Giddings, an instructor, and most likely to have been the leader of the formation, had briefed the pupils before the flight on the procedure for checking the oxygen flow to the mask. He had shown them the method, which involved squeezing the tube to the Type E mask being worn that day, a practice which had been forbidden for some time, owing to the possibility of damaging the economizer. The report on the accident stressed that this procedure must be prohibited, and the prohibition enforced.

The crater made by the crashing aircraft is still evident to this day. Moreover, Sergeant Sindelar's tragic passing has not gone entirely unremembered, for in May 1995 as part of the celebrations for the 50th Anniversary of V-E Day, the pupils of Rock School, encouraged by their teacher, Mrs Bosanquet, attempted to find out all they could about this wartime tragedy, which had happened so close to their school.

Vaclav Sindelar is buried at Chevington cemetery alongside his countryman Ladislay Kocourek.

### SERGEANT F.T.O. HULTON, RNZAF 05/05/1943

Sergeant Fergus Te-oha Hulton lost his life as the result of a mid-air collision, which was so dramatic that it is still remembered to this day (October 2001), by a number of people who lived in the Doddington and Horton areas east of Wooler at the time it occurred.

Fergus Hulton was born in Rotorua in 1923. His father, a Fijian Islander, died in 1930 leaving his mother, Isobel, to look after his upbringing alone.

He attended Rotorua High School and Wesley College, Pacrata, where he obtained his Higher School Leaving Certificate. He was a keen sportsman, playing not only for the Wesley College 1st XV Rugby Team, but also winning the School Boxing Championship at his weight.

When he first applied to join the RNZAF on 1st March 1941 he was employed as a clerk at the Native Department in Rotorua. He was enlisted as aircrew on 30th November 1941 at 1 Initial Training Wing, Levin, and commenced his flying training at 1 EFTS Taieri on 7th February 1942, before moving on to 2 SFTS, Woodbourne on 5th April. He gained his "wings" on 15th June, and was promoted to Sergeant on 5th September. This was shortly before he embarked for the UK on the 16th September, arriving at 3 PRC Bournemouth on the 18th November. It was now almost three months since he had flown an aircraft, and on 9th January 1943 he was posted to 2 EFTS at Worcester, for a short refresher course. On completion of this course on the 9th February, he was posted to 17 (P)AFU at RAF Watton.

He must have been there at the same time as Flight Sergeant Brown, and followed the latter to 57 OTU at Eshott, although there seems to be some confusion over the exact date of his transfer. Most records show the 23rd March, but one record gives 17th March, and yet another 24th April. As the vast majority of records show 23rd March, then it is most probably the correct date of his transfer.

With six training airfields and an operational airfield in the locality, the skies above the Borders must have been very busy indeed. And mid-air collisions were a frequent occurrence, but mostly between aircraft of the same unit.

So the mid-air collision, which took place on Wednesday 5th May 1943, was unusual in that it involved aircraft from two different units. At 15.03 that afternoon a formation of Spitfires, from 57 OTU at Eshott, including P7902, which was being flown by Sergeant Hulton, encountered a formation of Hurricanes from 59 OTU at Milfield. This encounter took place over the Doddington/Horton Moor area. The leader of the Hurricane formation, Flight Sergeant H.A. de Freitas flying AG111, decided that an impromptu mock attack on the Spitfires was in order, and dived on to their formation. Sergeant Hulton then committed a flagrant breach of flying discipline, and in response to the action of the Hurricane, broke away from the Spitfire formation and a general melee then ensued, during which the aircraft being flown by Sergeant Hulton (Spitfire P7902) and Flight Sergeant de Freitas (Hurricane AG111) collided, and fell to the ground out of control. The Hurricane crashed close to Doddington village, whilst the Spitfire is described as crashing closer to Wooler. Both pilots were killed instantly. Sergeant Hulton had completed 176 hours of flying in total, of which 33 had been spent flying Spitfires. He was buried at Chevington cemetery on Monday 10th May 1943.

## SERGEANT G.R. DAWSON RAFVR 02/06/1943

On Wednesday 2nd June 1943, Frank Moscrop, the young shepherd responsible for the more northerly parts of Auchope Farm, had reached the northernmost extremity of the farm, where it bounded Currburn at the head of a small steep sided valley, known locally at the time as Auchope Sike. The area is about three-quarters of a mile due south of the summit of the Curr, and about the same distance west of a hill known as the Black Hagg. Frank remembers thinking to himself how fortunate he was to have avoided the lambing, because the 'cuts' of the hill he shepherded, only carried 'eild' (barren) stock in the form of young replacement ewes. As he was musing on these thoughts, an aircraft appeared from the east only a few feet above the ground. Frank assumed it to be 'hedge hopping', but after it had disappeared from his view, there was a dull thud and the sound of the engine ceased. Frank carried on in the direction he though the final sounds had come from. Some time later he found the aircraft, which had apparently struck the ground once, bounced and then dived into the ground at about 60 degrees.

The pilot, Sergeant G.R. Dawson, had been partially thrown from the cockpit, and was lying over the leading edge of the remains of the wing of the aircraft. There had been a small fire, which had already gone out, and this had burnt some of the pilot's clothing, Frank having already ascertained that he was dead, and beyond help. The aircraft was Hurricane V 6860. The crash occurred at 13.40, and the aircraft had been in the air for just 5 minutes.

George Robert Dawson was born on the 16th July 1919 in Sao Paulo, Brazil, the son of William Rae and Mary Dawson. He enlisted in the RAF on 21st July 1941, but no details of his subsequent service and training are available. Sergeant Dawson must have only just been transferred to 59 OTU at the time, as he only had 145 hours of flying in total, of which only 9 hours were on Hurricanes. These nine hours would have been accumulated whilst with 59 OTU at Milfield. Hence the assumption that he must not have been there for very long.

He is buried in St Gregory's Churchyard, Kirknewton.

## SERGEANT D.H. MATHESON, RCAF 04/06/1943

Yet another aircraft collision was to claim the life of Sergeant Douglas Haig Matheson, but on this occasion the mishap took place on the ground.

Douglas Matheson, a native of Calgary, enlisted in the RCAF on 8th February 1940, but not as potential aircrew. His trade was given as "General Duties", and on 10th February he was taken on the strength of 119(BR) Squadron at Vancouver. This was a Canadian based Squadron, its number being entirely separate from the RAF sequence of squadron numbers (which the later "400" series of RCAF Squadrons were not), and operated Bolingbroke medium bombers (a Canadian built version of the Blenheim IV). AC2 Matheson, however, had nothing at all to do with the flying of these aircraft. In fact he must have been under training as a cook, because by the 4th November 1940 his trade was described as that, and he passed a test as a cook on the same date. On 1st January 1941 he was promoted to AC1, and on 1st April his trade was upgraded from cook 'C' to cook 'B'. He was to remain a cook for just over a year, and on 26th April 1942 he left 119(BR) Squadron and entered 3 Initial Training School, Victousville, Quebec. He was still there on 20th June, when his official "trade" was re-designated as "under training pilot". On 2nd August he started his flying training in earnest at 11 EFTS, Cap de la Madeleine, Quebec, and remained there until 25th October, when he was transferred to 13 SFTS St Hubert also in Quebec. It is not altogether clear when Douglas Matheson gained his "wings", but it would seem most probable that this was on 19th February 1943, as that was the day he was promoted to Sergeant. The two events usually went hand in hand, as the official policy of all the Commonwealth Air Forces (including the RAF) was that all qualified aircrew should have a minimum rank of Sergeant.

On 6th March Sergeant Matheson was at 'Y' Depot, Halifax awaiting embarkation for the UK. His dates of departure from Halifax and subsequent arrival in the UK are not recorded, but by early June he was undergoing his operational training at 57 OTU, Eshott.

Details of the accident in which he lost his life are sketchy, and not very precise. What is certain is that the accident occurred at 11.15, and that one of the aircraft involved had just returned from a flight, which had lasted 45 minutes. The two aircraft involved were Spitfire Is N3163 and X4896, and it is most likely that Sergeant Matheson was the pilot of the latter. The other pilot involved was Sergeant Q.E. Turton. One of the aircraft, although it is not clear which, but probably X4896, was stationary on the runway, when it was struck by the other aircraft, presumably N3163. The moving aircraft must have been moving quite fast, probably either taking off or landing, as in the resulting crash X4896 became a total write off, and N3163 was severely damaged. But more sadly, Sergeant Matheson was killed. He had completed a total of 197 hours of flying of which 15 hours had been spent flying Spitfires. He is buried at Chevington cemetery, now becoming the last resting place of increasing numbers of 57 OTU pupil pilots.


## FLIGHT SERGEANT T. COSSON, RNZAF 09/06/1943

The Mark II Beaufighter was to be responsible for yet another fatal casualty. This time, however, it was not the infamous swing, which caused the accident, but an engine failure, and the victim was a New Zealander.

Terence Cosson was born in Awanui, Auckland on the 5th December 1919. He received his secondary education at Kataia District High School, and on leaving School became a process worker. In March 1941 he was accepted for service in the RNZAF, having made an unsuccessful application in July 1939. He enlisted at the Initial Training Wing at Levin on the 21st December 1941, and from there was posted to 3 EFTS Harewood on the 9th February 1942. A further posting to 3 SFTS at Wigram came on the 2nd May 1942, and it was here on the 27th July that he was awarded his "wings". His training at Harewood and Wigram had been carried out on Tiger Moths and Oxfords respectively. Having enlisted as a LAC he was promoted to Sergeant on the 17th October, and on 23rd November embarked for the United Kingdom, arriving at 11 Personnel Despatch and Reception Centre, Brighton on the 23rd January 1943. He was posted to 12 (P)AFU RAF Grantham on the 4th March, and arrived at 54 OTU Charterhall on the 18th May. Once there he commenced his training on Beaufighters, and was promoted to Flight Sergeant on the 1st June.

On Wednesday 9th June Flight Sergeant Cosson was carrying out a daylight training flight in Beaufighter V8163. He had taken off from Winfield airfield, but at 10.45 the port engine seized due to lack of oil (or oil pressure). By this time the aircraft was not too far from Charterhall airfield, and Flight Sergeant Cosson elected to return there and attempt to land. However, the attempt at landing was not too successful and the aircraft struck the ground very heavily, damaging the undercarriage and bursting one of the tyres. Flight Sergeant Cosson immediately opened the throttles, and appeared to climb away under full control. But smoke and vapour started to appear from the port engine, which must have run long enough again for the climb away. At 2000 to 2500 feet the engine must have failed completely, and the aircraft started to spin to port. The aircraft crashed in the "Mid-Popering" Field about half a mile from the main steading at East Printonian Farm near Leitholm. Constable James Anderson of the Berwickshire Police attended the scene, and noted that the pilot of the aircraft was dead.

The arrangements for Terence Cosson's funeral, which was held at mid-day on Saturday 12th June at Fogo Churchyard, were made by the Station Commanding Officer, Group Captain R.H.A. Leigh. These arrangements, which included all the pall bearers being New Zealanders, were confirmed by Terence Cosson's sister, a Miss P. Cosson, who at the time was living in West Norwood, London.


### WARRANT OFFICER D.M. FLACK, RCAF 29/06/1943

An unexplained period of almost six months during which Donald Mitchell Flack was on indefinite leave without pay, made his passage through his early flying training a protracted process.

He first enlisted in the RCAF at Ottawa on 11th July 1941. After passing through several initial training units including No. 6 Bombing and Gunnery School at Mountain View, Ontario he was accepted as an under training pilot on 26th October 1941, and posted to 3 EFTS at London, Ontario. He was promoted from AC2 to LAC on the same day. At this unit Donald Flack would have learnt the rudiments of flying, using a Fleet Finch basic trainer aircraft. By the 21$^{st}$ December 1941he must have been thought to be competent enough to carry out more advanced flying, and was posted to 14 SFTS at Aylmer, Ontario. It is not clear when he gained his wings, but as he was promoted to Sergeant on 10th April 1942, it was probably on or close to that date. On the very next day, 11th April he was posted to 'Y' Depot, Halifax obviously with the intention of him coming to the UK to complete his operational training. However, this posting was amended, and on 12th April he was taken on the strength of 2 SFTS at Uplands, Ontario. What may have been instrumental in this decision is that on the same day, that is 12th April, he was admitted to the Station hospital, and he did not return to duty until the 12th May. The reason for his hospitalisation is not known, but whatever it was must have been fairly serious for him to have remained in hospital for a whole month. This might have been the reason for what happened next, which was a posting to 1 AOS at Malton, Ontario on 3$^{rd}$ June, followed by an immediate granting of "indefinite leave without pay". He was recalled to duty at 1 AOS on 20th November. This was a school for the training of navigators, and it is therefore a reasonable assumption that his brief period there was for administrative ("on strength pending disposal") reasons only. In fact, on the very next day he was transferred to 1 OTU at Bagotville, Quebec. Donald Flack stayed at 1 OTU until 27$^{th}$ March 1943, when he was transferred to 'Y' Depot at Halifax. He was struck off strength there on 7th April 1943, which was probably his date of embarkation for the UK.

The date of his arrival in the UK is not known, and neither are any details of his movements, but by the end of June 1943 he was serving with 59 OTU stationed at RAF Milfield.

On Tuesday 29th June 1943 W.O. Flack strapped himself into Hurricane P3715 at Brunton airfield. The weather was fine and clear, there being no cloud and with only a light northerly wind blowing. The time was probably around about 14.25 hours when he took off.

The object of the flight was to practice aerobatics at an altitude of 7,000 to 10,000 feet. Some 10 minutes after take-off, the aircraft was seen flying at an altitude of about 150 feet near Moussen Hill 6 miles north of Brunton. A loud backfire was heard and a puff of smoke was seen halfway between the propeller and the cockpit. The aircraft then side slipped down wind for 200 yards, before suddenly making a diving turn to port, resulting in it hitting the ground at high speed. W.O. Flack was killed instantly.

Because of the inexplicable nature of the crash, the wreckage was inspected by the Air Investigation Branch from Farnborough. The only mechanical defect which may have been responsible for the sudden turn to port were some sheared rivets in the starboard wing aileron differential control gear pulley, but the inspector's report stresses that it would be impossible to rule out that rivets may have been sheared as a result of the impact of the crash. But it also notes that the aircraft had been fitted with stressed alloy skin wings, as a replacement for the original fabric covered wings at 13 MU some months previously. During this procedure the differential control gear pulley was bound to have been worked on, and the inspector made a recommendation that the rivets in that pulley should be carefully checked in all Hurricanes, which had been modified in this way.

The conclusion of the report was that the initial problem was probably engine failure, which occurred at such a stage of flight (i.e. low altitude) that W.O. Flack's only chance of survival was to commit himself to a forced landing, which then went badly wrong, possibly because of the mechanical fault in the starboard aileron.

W.O. Flack was only 21 years old, and to have reached the rank of W.O.II by that age, especially considering the 6 months he had spent effectively out of the service, suggests that he was regarded as an above average airman. Neither did he lack experience, as he had completed 385 hours of flying in total, of which 83 hours had been in a Hurricane.

He was the victim of unfortunate circumstances, and now lies with his Commonwealth colleagues in St Gregory's Churchyard, Kirknewton.

# FLIGHT SERGEANT C.I. HUMPHREY, RNZAF 14/07/1943

Of the two airmen involved in yet another mid-air collision, one died instantly and the other, who survived the incident, was dead before the war came to an end.

Charles Ivan Humphrey was born at Timaru on 29th December 1921. He attended the Boy's High School there, passing his Matriculation Examination and taking an active part in both rugby and athletics. He stayed on at the school in order to try and gain his Higher Leaving Certificate, but at the same time took a part time job with the Timaru Herald newspaper. He applied to join the RNZAF on the 16th July 1940, and was accepted, although he did not sign his attestation document until 13th May 1941. At that time it was noted that he was declared temporarily unfit for service with the RNZAF, and probably because of that factor did not start his training at 1 ITW, Levin, until 9th February 1942. A fortnight later, still with the ITW, he was transferred to Rotorua, where he finished his initial training on 6th April 1942. Now he was to learn to fly, and moved to 1 EFTS, Taieri in order to do so. Here he flew on Tiger Moth aircraft, but on 16th June he was posted to 2 SFTS at Blenheim, where he continued his flying training, now on Harvard aircraft. He gained his "wings" on 2nd September, and was promoted to Sergeant on 28th November. He was granted pre-embarkation leave at the same time, and sailed for the UK on 6th January 1943, arriving on 11th February. The Personnel Despatch and Reception Centre at Bournemouth then became his home for almost three months, before finally being transferred to a flying unit, 17 (P)AFU now based at Wrexham on 4th May. His next move brought him to 59 OTU and RAF Milfield. This was on 8th June, one week after his promotion to Flight Sergeant.

Barely a month later on Wednesday 14th July at 09.55 hours Flight Sergeant Humphrey was flying Hurricane P3475 on a training flight, when he was in collision with another Hurricane, V7173, flown by P/O R.J. Currie RCAF. Flight Sergeant Humphrey's aircraft crashed to the ground at Church Farm Cottages, Elwick, and he was killed. Pilot Officer Currie was uninjured, and managed to land his aircraft back at Milfield. Unfortunately though, he did not survive the war, and he is buried in a military grave in Normandy.

By March 1944 Flying Officer Ronall James Currie was flying Hurricane IV's with 184 Squadron. The Squadron converted to Typhoons in April 1944, and on the 21st May 1944 Flying Officer Currie flew his first mission in a Typhoon against targets in the Turnhout area of Belgium. Although he did not fly any missions on D-Day, he did fly many times in the subsequent days, most of his missions being rocket projectile attacks against tanks and transport in the beachhead area. He does not appear to have been allotted an individual aircraft, but seems to have flown JR371 more often than any other aircraft.

On the 18th August 1944, whilst stationed at Airfield B5 at La Fresney, 184 Squadron was detailed to attack a concentration of German armour near the village of Trun, about 10 miles east of the town of Falaise. The squadron made three attacks during the day at 07.50, 13.15 and 16.00. During the attacks at 16.00 Flying Officer Currie's aircraft along with that of Flight Lieutenant Goss were seen to be hit by anti-aircraft fire, and then crash in flames behind enemy lines.

Flight Sergeant Humphrey lies in St Gregory's Churchyard, Kirknewton.

His next of kin was his foster sister, and it is believed that he may have been an orphan at the time of his enlistment into the RNZAF. He was certainly the child of a single-parent family, but it was his guardian, Mrs Lottie Bonnewith, rather than his natural mother, who gave consent for him to join the RNZAF.

**Headstone of Flight Sergeant Humphrey.**
**(Photo: The Author).**

88

# PETTY OFFICER (AIRMAN) A.H.P. ARCHIBALD, RNZN
## 19/07/1943

The impression given by the Charterhall (54 OTU) ORB is that Fairy Barracuda DP868 crashed either on or very close to the airfield at Charterhall on Monday 19th July 1943. In the same document the cause of the crash is given as engine failure.

However, with regard to the location of the crash, nothing could be farther from the truth. At18.26 that day Police Constable Andrew Wood reported the crash of this aircraft at the Longbank Field, Butterdean Farm, Grantshouse. A witness, James Dougal, of Quixwood, had seen the aircraft approaching, flying in a northerly direction. The engine was spluttering, and the aircraft was at a very low altitude. Suddenly the aircraft banked sharply to the left, and in so doing the port wing tip hit the ground. The aircraft did not recover from this encounter with mother earth, and smashed into the ground farther up the field. The pilot, Petty Officer(Airman) Arthur Herbert Percy Archibald, RNZN was killed.

Petty Officer Archibald applied to the RNZAF to serve as aircrew on 22nd June 1940. It is not clear whether he was turned down, or his application was passed on the RNZN, as the next record of him is his enlistment into the Navy on 28th August 1941. There is no information available regarding his training period, other than at the date of enlistment he was stationed at HMS St Vincent (probably a shore establishment). His nominal posting at the time of his death was to HMS Daedalus, although he was actually serving with 781 Squadron.

Like many other of the New Zealanders in this guide, he had been a keen sportsman whilst attending Royal Oak School and Sedden Memorial Technical College, both in the Auckland suburb of Royal Oak, close to his home at Three Kings. He had, however, been born at Optiki. At the time of his enlistment he was employed as a cashier.

The flight that day had started from RNAS Worthy Down, an establishment which stored, prepared and distributed aircraft to Fleet Air Arm (FAA) flying units. As Petty Officer Archibald was serving with 781 Squadron then, it is probable that he was delivering the Barracuda, a torpedo bomber and a particularly ugly and ungainly aircraft to look at, to that unit somewhere in Scotland, but that can only be conjecture.

Today he lies buried in the Churchyard at Fogo. On 1st March 1944 he would be joined by two more FAA aircrew, Sub-Lieutenant C. Newburgh-Hutchins and Sub-Lieutenant J.A. Luke, whose Fairy Fulmar X8696 crashed at Press Mains, Coldingham. The aircraft had taken off from the aircraft carrier HMS Pretoria Castle.

(Footnote:- HMS Daedalus was the Navy's name for the airfield at Lee-on-Solent, all Naval shore establishments being traditionally regarded as ships).

## FLIGHT SERGEANT W. ANDREW, RNZAF 27/07/1943

Like Sergeant Matheson RCAF, who had lost his life only seven weeks previously, Flight Sergeant Andrew was to be the victim of a collision on the ground. Once again the Mark II Beaufighter's difficult low speed handling characteristics were implicated in the cause of the crash.

Timaru, near Canterbury was not only Will Andrew's birthplace, but also where he was educated and where he was still living, when he enlisted in the RNZAF in September 1941. He had attended Timaru Boys High School where he gained a Senior Free Place (equivalent to 'O' level G.C.E.) in 1937. He later studied advanced drawing and commercial art whilst attending night classes at Timaru Technical College. He listed cricket, tennis, golf and miniature rifle shooting as his sporting interests. For a time he was employed as a sign writer by J. Ballantyne & Co of Timaru, before becoming self-employed in the same profession.

Like many New Zealanders who enlisted in the RNZAF his first posting was to the Initial Training Wing at Levin. He commenced his flying training at No. 1 EFTS Taieri on 29th November 1941, and made his first solo flight only a week later on the 6th December.

**Flight Sergeant W. Andrew RNZAF.
(Photo: New Zealand Defence Force
Archives).**

He was posted to Canada under the auspices of the BCATP on 14th January 1942, where he continued his flying training at 10 SFTS, Dauphin, Manitoba. He trained on Cessna Crane aircraft and was awarded his "wings" on the 5th June 1942. He was promoted to Sergeant on the same day having been a Leading Aircraftman (LAC) up to that time. By this time, as has been noted previously, it was the usual practice to promote all under-training other-rank aircrew to the rank of sergeant on becoming qualified.

Later in June he was posted for flying duties to No. 6 Bombing and Gunnery School, Mountainview, where he was probably involved in giving under-training air-bombers and air-gunners flying experience.

On 21st July he was posted to 2 SFTS at Uplands, Ontario where he was involved in flying duties in Avro Anson aircraft until 5th November, when he left for embarkation to the United Kingdom via the

91

now familiar "Y" Depot at Halifax. He disembarked in the UK on 1st December and went to the also now familiar 3 PRC at Bournemouth.

He was posted to 3 AFU at RAF South Cerney, in Gloucestershire on 12th January 1943, where he flew Airspeed Oxford aircraft. It is interesting to note that Sergeant Andrew's flying experience up to this point, including his elementary training, was virtually all in twin engined aircraft. It would appear, then, that it was always intended that he would fly either twin or multi-engined aircraft. Following a brief spell at 1515 Beam Approach Training Flight at RAF Swanton Morley during February, he was posted back to 3 AFU, but this time to its detachment at RAF Lulsgate Bottom in Somerset.

Bristol Blenheims were to become Sergeant Andrew's next aircraft type, when he was posted to 12 AFU at RAF Spitalgate near Grantham, early in April. Having concluded his course there and been promoted to Flight Sergeant, he was posted to 54 OTU at Charterhall on the 15th June.

On Tuesday 27th July 1943 Flight Sergeant Andrew was preparing to take off from Charterhall in Beaufighter II T3419. In the aircraft with him was Radar Operator/Observer Sergeant E.F. Edwards. As T3419 accelerated along the runway, it suddenly developed a swing, left the runway and hit a nearby blister hangar a glancing blow. This impact once again altered the course of the errant aircraft, and it sped off only to collide with Beaufort L4497, which was stationary. Flight Sergeant Andrew was killed instantly, but Sergeant Edwards only suffered slight injuries, a testimony, perhaps, to the inherent strength of the Beaufighter.

The cause of the vicious swing on take-off experienced by all types of Beaufighter was not solely aerodynamic The throttle controls were extremely sensitive, and pilots had to exercise maximum care in opening the throttles, so that both engines received the same increase in revs, otherwise a swing would be initiated, which because of the aerodynamic problem rapidly became worse.

Flight Sergeant Andrew had completed 530 hours of flying at the time of the accident. This amount of flying, together with the number of different types of aircraft flown would suggest that he certainly did not lack experience, a factor often blamed for flying accidents at Operational Training Units.

Will Andrew was buried at Fogo Church Cemetery, the second New Zealander to be so in as many weeks. The months of June and July had been a sad time for New Zealand in the Borders, four of its young airmen having been laid to rest.


## FLIGHT SERGEANT E.J.S. WILLIAMS, RAAF 19/09/1943

The demand for new and replacement aircrew was insatiable. So much so that the training programme at 54 OTU carried on with little heed to public holidays or weekends. Sundays were certainly not sacred, and Sunday the 19th September 1943 at RAF Winfield was definitely no exception.

At around 7.30pm on that day Beaufighter II T3360 took off on a routine training flight with Flight Sergeant F.J.V. McGrath from Perth, Western Australia at the controls. He had accumulated 196 hours of flying experience of which 44 hours had been spent flying Beaufighters. His Radio Navigator was Flight Sergeant Edward John Stacy Williams.

Flight Sergeant Williams was born in Perth on the 9th November 1911. He attended Hale College in Perth between 1924 and 1926. But by the time of his enlistment into the RAAF on the 7th November 1941, he was working and living in Hobart, Tasmania. It is not certain when he moved to Hobart, but it was probably not before 1931, because from 1928 until that year he served as a volunteer in the 44th Battalion of the Perth Militia, a territorial army unit.

He worked as a mine assayist prior to his enlistment in the RAAF. His first posting was to 1 ITS at Somers, where he received his basic military training. He had volunteered for aircrew training, and his

**Flight Sergeant E.J.S. Williams RAAF.**
**(Photo: National Archive of Australia).**

next posting on the 30th April 1942 was to 1 AOS at RAAF Cootamundra, New South Wales, where he would start to learn the rudiments of navigation in the air. RAAF West Sale and 3 BAGS were LAC Williams' next posting, where he arrived on the 28th August. On the 17th September he was awarded his Air Observer's brevet (service term for the half-wing badge awarded to aircrew other than pilots - Air Observer became Navigator later in the War). Four days later he was transferred to 1 ANS and was promoted to Sergeant on the 15th October. The next day he was posted to 5 Embarkation Depot in Fremantle. However, he did not leave Australia from there, but from 1 Embarkation Depot at Ascot Vale, where he had arrived on the 17th November. The records of his service are a trifle confused around this period, but the most likely date of his departure from Australia was the 15th January 1943. He arrived at 11 PRC in the UK on the 15th March. Although the route he travelled is not recorded, he must have come to the UK via USA and Canada, as he was court martialled for a very minor offence of military indiscipline at Camp Myles Standish in the USA.

Many of the Personnel Reception Centres (PRCs) were based in seaside holiday resort towns, making use of the redundant hotel accommodation. 11 PRC was no exception and like 3 PRC was based in and around Bournemouth. Sergeant Williams spent nearly four months at 11 PRC before being posted to 62 OTU at RAF Usworth on the 12th July, and during this time he met, and became engaged to Hazel, a young lady from Branksome Park, near Bournemouth. Also during this period, on the 15th April he was promoted to Flight Sergeant.

62 OTU specialised in the training of Interception by Radio Direction Finding (i.e.radar) techniques, and had been formed from a flight of 3 Radio Direction Finding School in June 1942.

On the 4th September Flight Sergeant Williams married Hazel. Their honeymoon, if they had one at all, must have been brief, for on the 7th September he was posted to 54 OTU at Charterhall. Certainly there is no evidence that he was awarded any leave at the time, although it is known that the No. 25 Course he attended at 62 Operational Training Unit came to an end on 28th August.

So when Beaufighter T3361 took off that night, Flight Sergeant Williams had only been married for two weeks and spent only eleven days at Charterhall.

At 21.09 Flight Sergeant McGrath was circling Winfield airfield looking for another aircraft, when he reported that one of his aircraft's engines was on fire, and that he and Flight Sergeant Williams were preparing to abandon the aircraft. Six minutes later the aircraft crashed at Langton Lees, Harden's Farm, near Duns, and burst into flames. The local National Fire Service unit attended the blaze, which was finally extinguished at quarter past midnight, when it was discovered that the crew had not carried out their intentions. Flight Sergeant McGrath's body was found 150 yards from the wreckage, whilst Flight Sergeant Williams' body was trapped in the remains of his cockpit. A subsequent RAF enquiry could not establish any reason why the crew had not used their parachutes to abandon the aircraft.

The Beaufighter they had been flying, T3361, had completed 386 hours of flying and so could not be considered to have been worn out. Indeed the port Rolls-Royce Merlin engine had only completed 154 hours of running since it had been installed as a replacement on the 6th June 1943, whilst the starboard engine had merely 108 hours of use since its installation on 4$^{th}$ July.

The cause of the engine fire was either not established. Or if it was, then it was not recorded.

Flight Sergeant Williams was buried in Fogo Churchyard at 12 noon on Friday 24$^{th}$ September with full service honours. Whether Hazel Williams attended the funeral is not clear, but that she was a bride for only two weeks before becoming a widow needs no clarification.


## FLYING OFFICER G.W. BIGMORE, RAAF 18/10/1943

The Merlin engined Beaufighter was to claim yet another antipodean victim, the third in as many months, in October 1943. Once again the aircraft involved was operating with 54 OTU at Charterhall, but on this occasion the difficult handling characteristics at low airspeed of the Beaufighter were not in any way implicated as the cause of the accident.

Flying Officer Gordon William Bigmore; an Australian whose hometown was Malvern, Victoria arrived at Charterhall on the 7th September 1943. He had been working as an insurance clerk, when he enlisted in the RAAF on the 25th April 1942. He was already serving as a reservist in the Victoria Scottish Regiment Militia, but was released from his commitment to that unit as soon as he signed up for the RAAF. His initial training (i.e. drill, discipline and general military life) took place at 1 ITS Somers. He moved on to 7 EFTS at Western Junction on 5th August, where he received his first flying training in Tiger Moths, as part of Course No. 27. He was clearly a quick learner, because on 22nd October he was transferred to 1 SFTS at Point Cook, where he was introduced to flying twin engined aircraft in the shape of Airspeed Oxfords. His progress must have been good, as he was awarded his "wings" on 11th February 1943, and on the same day was commissioned as a Pilot Officer. On the next day he was transferred to 1 Embarkation Depot in Melbourne, and on 6th March he left there to start his long journey to the UK. This journey was via the USA and Canada, leaving San Francisco on 22nd March. He arrived at Camp Myles Standish on 27th March, where he stayed along with other Australian airmen until the 7th April. The whole draft of Australian airmen then entrained for Halifax, arriving there on the 9th April. They embarked the same day, and arrived at Liverpool on the 17th April. Pilot Officer Bigmore was posted to 11 PDRC the next day, and stayed there until posted to 12 (P)AFU Grantham on the 8th June. Here he received more advanced flying instruction, and was also promoted to Flying Officer on the 11th August. Having completed this course he then moved to Charterhall.

By the time he took off in Beaufighter T3428 on the evening of Monday 18th October, Flying Officer Bigmore had accumulated 174 hours of flying in total. However, only 27 hours of this had been spent flying a Beaufighter, and more importantly, of only 15 hours spent flying at night, merely 7 hours had been in a Beaufighter.

Together with his Navigator/Radio Operator, Flying Officer Hirst, Flying Officer Bigmore had been airborne for 2 hours and 25 minutes, when he began to make his preparations to land at Charterhall at around 22.00 hours When he had taken off the weather had been clear and fine, but at 21.00 hours a bank of low cloud had been blown in by a light south easterly wind. In order to try and establish his position accurately Flying Officer Bigmore made a wider than normal circuit in his approach to land, but in so doing flew into a hill, which was obscured by the low cloud. This hill was approximately 3 miles north west of Greenlaw. The aircraft burst into flames. Flying Officer Bigmore was killed, and Flying Officer Hirst very seriously injured. A report on the accident states that all pilots at 54 OTU had to take an exam on the local topography, before they were allowed to fly. A suggestion was also made that the officer in charge of the night flying operations should have a minimum rank of Flight

Lieutenant, which indicates that the officer in charge on the night of 18th October may have had a more junior rank, and probably less experience than the responsibility demanded.

Flying Officer Bigmore, who was 21, joined his fellow Australians already at rest in Fogo Churchyard.

Before the war came to an end they would be joined by yet another.

### FLYING OFFICER U.L. LOOK-YAN RAFVR 14/01/1944

In July 2000 a small plaque commemorating the death of Ulric Leslie Look-Yan was placed at the entrance to the steading at Roseden Farm. This farm, about 6 miles south of Wooler, was the scene of the crash of a Hurricane IIB, Z3076, which was being flown by Flying Officer Look-Yan. The aircraft was on the strength of 59 OTU at RAF Milfield, and the accident occurred on the 14th January 1944.

Ulric Leslie Look-Yan was a member of the Chinese community in Trinidad. This community was closely involved in the business and social structure of the island, and had become established in the late 1850s, when Chinese labourers were indentured to work on Trinidad's sugar plantations, in order to rectify

**Flying Officer U.L Look-Yan. (Photo: Look-Yan family via K.Davies).**

the labour shortage created by the abolition of slavery. Born in 1922 in the Port of Spain, "Lin", as Ulric was known by his family, started his

**Flying Officer U.L Look-Yan in D.H. Tiger Moth, probably at RAF Netherravon.**
**(Photo: Look-Yan family, via K. Davies).**

training as a pilot under the Trinidad Air Training Scheme on the 28th March 1942. At this time he held the rank of Leading Aircraftman and still held this rank when posted to 41 Service Flying Training School, Moncton, Canada, under the auspices of the BCATP on the 28th July 1942.

He competed his course of training in November 1942, having made his first solo flight in June 1942. He was awarded his pilots "wings" on the 30th November, and shortly afterwards on the 3rd December was discharged from service in the ranks, on being commissioned as Pilot Officer. He embarked for the UK almost immediately, and arrived at 7 Personnel Receiving Centre on the 27th January 1943.

He was not posted to a flying unit until the 11th May, which suggests that BCATP was being more successful than had been envisaged, and more pilots were being produced than the Advanced Flying Training Programme could absorb. That posting was to 5 (Pilots) Advanced Flying Unit at RAF Ternhill.

On the 4th June he was promoted to the rank of Flying Officer, and on completion of his course at 5 (P)AFU on the 29th June, was transferred to the Glider Pilot Exercise Unit at RAF Netheravon. He arrived there in the company of seven other RAF pilots, two officers and five sergeants. They were to become staff pilots, giving flying experience to army personnel being trained as glider pilots. Their remit was not to instruct these under training glider pilots, but merely to give them the necessary flying experience in their intensive training programme. The aircraft used were mostly Tiger Moth biplanes, but occasional flights were carried out using Miles Masters. On the 29th July Flying Officer Look-Yan made a successful "wheels-up" landing on Netheravon airfield in Master EN386, and it is assumed that the undercarriage must have failed, as no mention of pilot error or other cause is made in the report of this incident. In early October the whole unit was transferred to RAF Thruxton for 10 days, while a major training exercise was carried out.

Having returned to Netheravon Flying Officer Look-Yan's stay there was not destined to last much longer, and he was transferred to 59 OTU at RAF Milfield on the 30th November. Shortly after this the Glider Pilot Exercise Unit was disbanded. Only four days after arriving at Milfield, on the 4th December, "Lin" was flying Hurricane T9534 when it was involved in a flying accident. There is a possibility that this may have been "Lins" first flight in a Hurricane. It must have only been a minor accident, as there is no record of any injuries being caused, and neither is there a record of any damage to the aircraft.

Sometime late in the morning of Friday 14th January 1944 Flying Officer Look-Yan strapped himself into the cockpit of Hurricane IIB Z3076. There was a gusty wind blowing, but conditions were not considered unsuitable for flying.

The aircraft was a veteran of 629 hours of flying. It had first been issued to 242 Squadron in April 1941. The aircraft became the regular mount of Pilot Officer D.M. Hicks, an Australian, and on the 17th June 1941, he became involved in a dog-fight with several Me 109s over the northern French town of Bethune whilst flying Z3076. As a result of this action one Me 109 was claimed as being damaged. A similar action in the same area took place on the 4th July, which once again involved Pilot

100

Officer Hicks flying Z3076, and resulting in another Me 109 being badly damaged. However, on the 17th August, whilst being flown by Sergeant Sands, Z3076 was involved, together with five other Hurricanes of 242 Squadron in a dog-fight with a formation of Me 109s. This action resulted in two of the Me 109s being destroyed. Pilot Officer Hicks, who on this occasion was flying Hurricane Z3845, was posted "missing" after this action. On the 30th August Z3076 was flown by Sergeant John Manby as escort to a Blenheim formation attacking shipping off the Belgian coast near Ostend. By a strange quirk of fate Sergeant Manby lost his life in the Borders during early October 1941, when the Hurricane he was flying, Z2349, crashed into high ground near Riccarton Junction (refer to a "Border Too High" for full story). The aircraft was being ferried from RAF Valley in Anglesey to RAF Turnhouse near Edinburgh. By this time 242 Squadron had been disbanded in the UK, and had relinquished both Z3076 and Sergeant Manby. During its stay with 242 Squadron Z3076 had been operated from RAF stations, Stapleford Tawney, North Weald, and Manston.

The aircraft then passed to 121 Squadron based at RAF Kirton-in-Lindsey on the 1st September. It was test flown by Pilot Officer Geffene on 2nd September and he and Pilot Officer Edner seemed to have shared the use of the aircraft during most of that month. From then on Z3076 appears to have been flown by nearly every pilot serving with the squadron. On the 20th October the squadron converted to Spitfires, and Z3076 became surplus to requirements. It was transferred to 253 Squadron based at RAF Hibaldstow on the 29th October, but was not flown until the 7th December, when Lieutenant Loken, a Norwegian, was at the controls. He was not to fly the aircraft again, as he was posted missing on the 12th December.

The aircraft was involved in a minor accident on the 19th January 1942, and was repaired at RAF Hibaldstow on the 2nd February by the Civilian Repair Organisation. It was returned for use again on the 6th February. 253 Squadron's main activity seemed to be convoy patrols, and the majority of these were uneventful. That they were mostly without incident bears out the effectiveness of operating standing air patrols above convoys. Attacks by either aircraft or naval vessels, including submarines, were definitely deterred. However, on the 20th February,

Z3076 was in action whilst being flown by Sergeant J.H. Stitt. Throughout the Spring and Summer of 1942, 253 Squadron and Z3076 activities followed this routine, the only variation being the use of different airfields as home base. As well as RAF Hibaldstow the squadron was based at Shoreham and Friston.

Z3076 was transferred to 245 Squadron on the 22nd September. This squadron was part of the newly formed 2nd Tactical Air Force, and was based at RAF Middle Wallop. The aircraft's first, and only, operational flight with this squadron was on the 8th October, when it was flown by Sergeant D. Maxwell. Although the aircraft is officially shown as remaining on the strength of this squadron until the 20th July 1943, its use must have been very limited, as the unit converted to Typhoons in February 1943.

Z3076 arrived at RAF Milfield, and its final operator 59 OTU on the 20th July.

The object of Flying Officer Look-Yan's flight in the veteran Z3076 that day was low-level cross country training. At around 12.15pm he was returning to Milfield just before the children attending Roddam School had commenced their lunch break. Diana Walton, whose parents farmed and lived at Roseden Farm, was among a group of children from the school, who were walking back to Roseden for their lunch. Their journey would take them along the track which ran due north from the school before joining the Roseden to Roddam road, where it crossed the Roddam Burn.

At some point in their journey Hurricane Z3076 passed overhead at a very low altitude. Diana Walton, even to the present day, is convinced that the aircraft was on fire. It must have been in some kind of trouble, however, because one of the other children in the group, the Roseden shepherd's son, remarked to Diana, "I hope that lands on your hoos!" And it very nearly did. It struck a glancing blow to the ground about 100 metres to the south of Roseden Farmhouse, and then careered on out of control, before hitting the large tree at the rear entranceway to the farmhouse. It finally came to rest between a Dutch barn and some other farm buildings, only narrowly missing the latter. Nowadays this area is the car park for The Roseden Farm Shop. Some Land Army girls were working in these buildings, and were lucky to escape injury as pieces of wreckage ricochetted in all directions. Flying Officer Look-Yan was left suspended in the tree by his harness, and it was soon established that he had not survived the crash.

The large parts of the wreckage of the aircraft were removed almost immediately by personnel from RAF Milfield, although Italian prisoners-of-war were on site for some time clearing up the smaller pieces of detritus.

Ulric Leslie Look-Yan was laid to rest in Stonefall Cemetery, Harrogate on Thursday 20th January 1944, the funeral service being conducted by the Roman Catholic Chaplain. His family were represented by a Mr Achong, a cousin of his mother, together with his wife, who at the time were living in Rochdale. The reasons for his interment at Harrogate rather than at St Gregory's Churchyard, Kirknewton, alongside other Commonwealth airmen, who died while serving at RAF Milfield, are not clear, but may have been because he was a member of the Roman Catholic faith.

**Funeral of U. L. Look-Yan at Stonefall Cemetary, Harrogate. (Photo: Look-Yan family via K. Davies).**

In the Spring of 2000 a close neighbour of Diana Walton was fascinated by her account of the accident. He decided to find out more details regarding the incident, including the identity of the aircraft and its pilot, of which Diana Walton had no knowledge. By a strange train of coincidences the Look-Yan family were located, and it was at this time that it was decided that a small memorial plaque at the crash site would be a fitting tribute. As far as it is known, this is the only single memorial to an airman, other than a headstone, in the area.

## FLIGHT SERGEANT J.M. MORRIS RAF 07/03/1944

Almost two years had passed since RAF Acklington's previous Commonwealth casualty, when on Tuesday 7th March 1944 a Spitfire of 222 Squadron crashed whilst practising elementary aerobatics, killing its pilot Flight Sergeant John Malcolm Morris.

Born in Erdington, Birmingham in August 1922 John Malcolm Morris was a resident of Kenya by the time he enlisted in the RAF on 15th April 1941. His parents lived in Nairobi, and it is probable that his father was one of the ex-servicemen from World War I, who took up the offer of a new start in Kenya by the British Government at its expense.

Flight Sergeant Morris had completed a fair amount of operational flying before 222 Squadron moved to Acklington in January 1944. Most of this operational flying consisted of escorting light/medium bombers on daylight raids over Occupied Northern France and the Low Countries, and was carried out from RAF Hornchurch in Essex. He completed six flights in total during November 1943, two of these being on the same day, the 25th, when he flew Spitfire IX LF MH476 between 09.05 and 10.25 escorting Ramrod 330 and Spitfire IX LF MH732 escorting Ramrod 333 between 15.10 and 15.45. Both of these attacks were against the Audighem area of Belgium, Ramrod being the code name used for this type of attack by light/medium bombers escorted by large numbers of fighters. One of the objectives of these kinds of operations was to goad the Luftwaffe into defensive action, but the ruse very rarely worked. However, Ramrod 316 on 19th November had provoked the Luftwaffe into putting some aircraft into the air, and 222 Squadron including Flight Sergeant Morris flying Spitfire IX LF MH371 got into a brief dogfight with some Me109s over the target area. No Luftwaffe aircraft were damaged, however, and neither were any of the Spitfires of 222 Squadron. The squadron remained at Hornchurch until the end of December, and Flight Sergeant Morris completed two more operational missions during the month, one on the 5th December, flying Spitfire IX LF MJ150 and taking part in an attack on Saint Josse, and the other on 20th December, flying MH571 escorting 72 Marauder medium bombers in an attack against Abbeville.

222 Squadron came to Acklington on 25th February 1944. It was probably considered to be a rest period, as by this time the North East was experiencing very little enemy air activity. The squadron had come to Acklington from Hornchurch, where they had been on continuous operational duty since April 1943, and there had been brief postings to RAF Woodvale, near Liverpool and RAF Catterick before their arrival at Acklington. Although regarded as a rest period, training flights were still carried out, it being vitally important that the pilots were kept at the peak of their skills, especially with the invasion of Europe being imminent.

On Tuesday 7th March Flight Sergeant Morris was involved in some elementary aerobatic training near the moors to the west of Alnwick in Spitfire V EP660. His aircraft hit the top of some trees which were shrouded by mist, and then lost control, smashing through more pine trees, before crashing through a wall on the northern lip of the deep cutting of the Alnwick to Wooler railway (LNER) line just to the south of Lemmington Branch. Tommy Anderson who farmed at Overthwarts, a little further to the west, witnessed the crash. As the aircraft came to a halt, pieces broke off it and were scattering in all directions. One piece went tumbling and rolling at high speed across the short distance between the wall and the buildings at Lemmington Branch, and reached there at precisely the same moment that Sid Roundtree, the shepherd, appeared from around the corner of the buildings. The fast moving part of the Spitfire, believed to be an ammunition box or track, took his legs away from under him, breaking them in the process. The Spitfire also demolished a hut in which Mr Turner, the farmer at Lemmington Branch, had stored a caravan.

Sid Roundtree, although injured, survived the experience, but unfortunately Flight Sergeant Morris did not. He was buried at Chevington Cemetery at 13.45 on Thursday 9th March1944. Flight Lieutenant Varley had been in charge of the funeral arrangements. The next day, the 10th March, 222 Squadron returned to Hornchurch, leaving behind a poignant reminder of their brief stay at Acklington.

But even in 2002 that headstone is not the only reminder of John Malcolm Morris's passing, for the rebuilt part of the wall, where his Spitfire crashed, is still easily distinguishable from the rest.


## WARRANT OFFICER H.A. DOUGLAS, RAAF 17/03/1944

Although losing his life whilst posted to a training unit, Hamilton Alexander Douglas was on the staff of 54 OTU at Charterhall and not a student.

The son of an accountant he was born at Rockhampton, Queensland, Australia on 18th July 1922. At the time of his enlistment into the RAAF on the 21st June 1941, he was employed as a Bank Clerk in the small town of Mackay in Queensland. He had been a diligent scholar at both Mackay Intermediate State School and All Souls School, Charters Towers, passing six subjects in his Junior Public Examination and a further four in his State Scholarship Examination.

Although he was employed as a Bank Clerk with Union Bank of Australia at the time of his enlistment, he had been studying accountancy with Homingway and Robertson, in Brisbane. Early in 1940 he had joined the Mackay Militia as a Cadet.

On enlistment he was posted to 3 ITS Sandgate, where he stayed until 15th October 1941, when he was posted to 2 EFTS at Archerfield to commence his flying training. He must have made good progress and was transferred to 2 SFTS at Wagga on 9th December. He attained the rank of LAC on the 9th September 1941, gained his "wings" on the 6th March 1942, and was then posted to 5 SFTS at Uranquinty on the 2nd April for a bayonet course, during which he was promoted to Sergeant on the 30th April.

He passed through two Embarkation depots, No. 3 at Sandgate and No. 2 at Bradfield Park, and finally left Australia, bound for the UK on the 2nd July. Like so many of the other young men in this guide, his first posting on arrival in Britain was to 3 PRC at Bournemouth on 18th August. His first flying posting in the UK was to 5 (P)AFU at Ternhill on the 1st September. On the 22nd September he was transferred to 53 OTU at Llandow in South Wales, a unit equipped with Spitfires, and was promoted to Flight Sergeant on the 30th October.

On the 12th December 1942 Flight Sergeant Douglas took off from Llandow in Spitfire IIA P7442. The time was around 11.15 and the purpose of the flight was further flying experience for Flight Sergeant Douglas, who by this time had accumulated 147 hours of flying in total, with 56 of these being in control of a Spitfire. Around an hour and a half later at 12.45, the aircraft had crossed the estuary of the River Seven and was over the county of Gloucester. Flight Sergeant Douglas reported over the R/T, that he was experiencing trouble with the throttle of the Merlin engine, and was about to make a forced landing. This must have gone badly wrong for the aircraft crashed at Waterend Farm, Coaley, near Cambridge (Glos). The crash must have been very serious, as the damage to both aircraft and engine was assessed as Category 'E', that is a "write off". Flight Sergeant Douglas's injuries must also have been very serious, as he was admitted to the RAF hospital at Innsworth suffering from multiple injuries, and put on the dangerously ill list. He was removed from the dangerously ill list on the 19th December, and was transferred to Hartpury Cottage Hospital near Gloucester on the 9th February 1943.

On the 5th May he was finally removed from all sick lists and discharged from Innsworth.

His stay in hospital, however, seems to have caused a problem to those compiling his records, for there are only a few further mentions of his whereabouts, until a brief entry in the 54 OTU ORB reports his death on the 17th March 1944.

His recovery from his injuries was fairly protracted, as he was attached to two Airmen's Convalescent Units from the time of his discharge from hospital until the 28th September 1943. He must then have returned to 53 OTU, as his promotion from Flight Sergeant to Warrant Officer in October was authorised by that Unit. His presence at 54 OTU was only an "attachment", which commenced on 22nd December 1943, and he remained officially posted to 53 OTU.

The cause of his death is given as the crash of a Martinet Target Tug aircraft EM481 on take-off from Winfield. The aircraft crashed in the "Knowey Field," Horndean Farm at 14.30 hours, and was witnessed by Special Constable George Dean. The winch operator, LAC Bainbridge died of his injuries.

Although both RAF and local police reports record the crash as having occurred on Friday 17th March 1944, both the CWGC register and RAAF service files record Warrant Officer Douglas's death as having occurred on Saturday 18th March. Perhaps this discrepancy could be accounted for by his death occurring away from his officially posted unit. His headstone in Fogo Churchyard is dated 18th March. He was destined to be the last Australian laid to rest there.

## FLYING OFFICER J.W. VAN HAMEL RAFVR 11/04/1944

Jacob Wilhelm van Hamel, better known to his close friends as "Jaap" is the only Dutch airman to be buried in a Border grave. Indeed very few of those airmen from the occupied countries of Western Europe, who lost their lives in the Border area, still remain buried there.

Born in theHague in 1920 "Jaap" Van Hamel entered the University of Delft in 1937 to study civil engineering. Although he became a member of the University rowing club, he never excelled as an oarsman probably because of his very slight build. On 5th February 1940, he was conscripted into military service and subsequent to some officer training, became a corporal on 4th May 1940. In the early autumn of 1940 following the German occupation of Holland, he joined a resistance group run by Dr. J.A.A. Mekel of Delft. The main activity of this group was the collection of information concerning German military installations. The group was also instrumental in helping those Dutchmen who wished to carry on the fight against the Germans, and in order to do so, fled to Britain so that they could join the allied armed forces. Many of these young men crossed the North Sea by small (sometimes very small) boat, hence their collective name in Holland of "England Sailors".

On the 11th December 1940, Jan Bouwer, who had been a captain in the Dutch army reserve, was shot and killed at his home in Delft. There were suspicions that this man may have betrayed some of the "England Sailors" to the Gestapo. However, there were also suggestions that one of the perpetrators of this shooting, Hugo De Man, was also a traitor to the Mekel group, and that he carried out the slaying in order to take attention away from himself and strengthen his position within the

**J.W. Van Hamel (3rd from right) whilst under training in Canada. Note white stripe in cap denoting under-training aircrew of the BCATP.**
**(Photo: Mrs G. Grootshoff-Van-Hamel).**

Mekel group. His accomplice in the killing was "Jaap" van Hamel, who may not have been aware of De Man's treachery, but certainly was of Bouwer's. On 18th June 1941 De Man was arrested by the Gestapo for another, different offence. Under interrogation De Man confessed to the murder of Bouwer, which resulted in the Gestapo blackmailing him by promising not to execute him if he would reveal the names of the Mekel group. "Jaap" was now in grave danger. He and his friend, "Rudi" van Daaler Wetters, had already attempted to escape from Holland, but now that De Man had been arrested, it became essential that they left the country.

Their first attempt to escape was by stealing an aircraft, for which they had first to acquire a propeller, as the Germans had removed all propellers from Dutch aircraft after two other Dutchmen had escaped by plane several days previously. The attempt failed, however, as the plane refused to leave the ground.

They then decided to escape to Britain by sea, and to facilitate this, bought a canoe with a small outboard motor. In order that the German authorities did not find it, and also so that it was

J.W. Van Hamel at an unknown location, most likely to have been RAF Peterborough 5(P)AFV. Note sergeant's stripes and soccer posts, the latter indicating a UK location.
(Photo: Mrs G. Grootshoff-Van-Hamel).

Pilot Officer J.W. Van Hamel (standing 3rd from aircraft), with
Harvard Advanced Trainer, probably at 5(P)AFV.
(Photo: Mrs G. Grootshoff-Van-Hamel).

322 Squadron flying personnel whilst at No 12 Armament Practice
Camp at RAF Llanbedr, N Wales, in Nov. 1943. Flying Officer Van
Hamel 3rd from right, middle row.
(Photo: Mrs G. Grootshoff-Van-Hamel).

**Flying Officer J.W. Van Hamel on wing of Spitfire VB.**
**(Photo: Mrs G. Grootshoff-Van-Hamel).**

very close to the sea, they hid it in a small tunnel running through the dunes near the seaside resort of Katwijk. This tunnel was used for the transfer of sick and handicapped children in wheelchairs from their hospital (the "Zeehospitium") to the beach.

On the night of the 20th/21st June 1941 they assembled the canoe under cover of darkness, and with the help of two assistants launched it into the sea. They could not paddle, but relied on a small blue-green sail to propel them away from the shore, in order that the outboard motor would be out of earshot from the shore, before it was started. At the point where they thought it safe to attempt to start the motor, they did so, only for the motor to fail completely. They threw it overboard together with the tins of petrol brought along to complete the journey.

After 4 days at sea, during which time because of a shift in wind direction, they had to paddle considerable distances, they sighted a convoy. One of the convoy escorts, an Australian destroyer, H.M.S.

Eglinton, spotted them and picked them up. By then they had become very weak, and due to having been kept in the cramped, confined space of the canoe, had virtually lost the use of their legs, and had to sit on the deck of the destroyer, until the effects of a hot mug of tea liberally laced with rum, revived them.

They were landed at Lowestoft on 26th June 1941. Owing to the fact that their canoe had been made in Germany, they were viewed with some suspicion, and were interrogated at the Patriotic School in London for almost three weeks before some Dutch friends, who had arrived in England before them, interceded on their behalf.

"Jaap" was then sent to the Prinses Irene Brigade at Wrottesley Park near Wolverhampton. On the 18th August 1941 he was passed fit for aircrew, and two days later enlisted in the RAF at the Aircrew Reception Centre, Abbey Lodge, London.

He started his flying training at No. 1 EFTS Hatfield on 7th November 1941, and then moved on to No. 21 EFTS at Booker on 24th February 1942, where the training became more advanced. Both these units utilised Tiger Moth aircraft. On 9th May 1942 he went to Canada, probably as part of BCATP. He was stationed at Moose Jaw, where he received more advanced training on Harvard aircraft. He returned to Britain in November 1942, and was posted to an Advanced Flying Unit (AFU) at Peterborough flying Miles Masters. By now his training was at a very advanced stage indeed, and in January 1943 he was posted to 57 OTU at Eshott, to convert to flying Spitfires. He was promoted to Pilot Officer on 28th February 1943, and at the end of March 1943 was posted to 167 Squadron at RAF Ludham.

Between March 1943 and June 1943, 167 Squadron moved from RAF Ludham to RAF Digby, then to RAF Tangmere and finally to RAF Westhampnett, (Goodwood). During that time the squadron operated Spitfire Mark V's, and carried out fighter sweeps over the Low Countries. "Jaap" Van Hamel was involved in these operations, until his transfer to the newly formed all Dutch 322 (Nederland) Squadron in June 1943.

Initially this squadron was based at RAF Woodvale near Liverpool, and was involved in convoy patrols and reconnaissance flights, whilst working up to full operational status. At the end of December 1943 the squadron moved to RAF Hawkinge in Kent. There the squadron was used as escort to medium bomber formations attacking, during daylight, targets in the Low Countries and northern France. These missions frequently took place on a daily basis, and during January, February and early March "Jaap" Van Hamel flew 14 operational missions, mostly in Spitfire VB VL-C, but also in VL-H, VL-K (both Spitfire VB's) and VL-G (a Spitfire VC).

In mid March 1944 the Squadron moved to RAF Acklington to re-equip with Spitfire XIV's. The Commanding Officer of the Squadron at this time was Major Kuhlmann of the South African Air Force. He was probably appointed because of his ability to speak Afrikaans (similar to Dutch) and English, and thus be able to liase between British and Dutch personnel in the Squadron.

At this time the Squadron ORB makes references to some of the difficulties, which were being experienced in converting on to the new mark of aircraft. One of the problems encountered was a shortage of cartridges for the Coffman starter of the Griffon engine. This was overcome by trips to 57 OTU at Eshott to 'borrow' further supplies. This airfield, of course, was already known to "Jaap" Van Hamel, as he had done his original conversion to Spitfires there only a year previously.

The other difficulty mentioned frequently was a fault with the oxygen system on the new type of aircraft.

At about 16.15 hours on 11th April 1944 a soldier, Rifleman Seccombe of the Kings Royal Rifle Corps stationed in Rothbury, observed an aircraft with its engine going 'flat out'. (His description). It then entered a cloud only to re-emerge in an inverted dive. It appeared that it might pull out from this dive, but it did not and struck the hillside, disintegrated, and burst into a large sheet of flame. The aircraft had crashed just to the south of Great Tosson Farm, and the present farmer there Tom Snaith, remembers as a child, seeing the aircraft crash, whilst going on a shopping trip to Rothbury with his mother. "Jaap" Van Hamel was the unfortunate pilot involved in this crash. The cause of the accident was thought to be a failure of the oxygen system, following which the pilot 'blacked-out'. The aircraft involved in this incident was Spitfire XIV NH700, which had only been issued to the Squadron on the 14th March.

"Jaap" Van Hamel's funeral took place at 14.00 hours on 15th April 1944 at Chevington Cemetery. HM Queen Wihelmina was represented by Major Chaplain A.F.M. Monchen, and the Dutch Air Ministry by Captain Kamphuis.

The following eulogy appears, very unusually, in the Squadron's ORB.

"Our late friend was buried at the little Cemetery of Chevington, where other pilots are buried. Near the grave could be seen the names of pilots belonging to the Fighting French, Norwegian and other countries at present under Nazi yoke. A gallant lot of men, who, through the maze of unpredictable events have found their resting place in this part of Northern England along the North Sea. Good-bye Van Hamel, a good friend, a good companion. Many pilots remarked on the loss to the Squadron of such a keen and likeable pilot".

(signed)

Major Kuhlmann (CO)

(South African Air Force)

And the end of the story of a courageous, selfless and patriotic young man.

Flying Officer "Jaap" Van Hamel is also remembered on several memorials in his native Holland. Situated in a small chapel at Loenen (Gelderland) is a memorial to those "England Sailors", including Jaap Van Hamel, who subsequently lost their lives after crossing the North Sea. His name is also included on the commemorative panels in the main hall of the Delft Technical University,

**Original grave marker of Flying Officer J.W. Van Hamel immediately after the war. It erroneously showed him to have been serving in the Royal Netherlands Naval Airservice. (Photo: Mrs G. Grootshoff-Van-Hamel).**

and on a glass panel in the library of the "Delft Studenten Corps" Club. Both of these panels honour those former students who lost their lives in WW II.

## LIEUTENANT COMMANDER D.R.B. COSH, DSC, RCNVR
### 24/06/1944

In the north wall of the western end of the nave of St Gregory's Church, Kirknewton there is a beautiful stained glass window. The window is in two sections, with the left section, as viewed from inside the church, depicting a knight in blue armour holding a shield bearing the cross of St George. At the bottom of this section is the Royal

Air Force crest, and this part of the window commemorates all those airmen who lost their lives, whilst serving at RAF Milfield. The right section of the window depicts a knight in gold armour holding a large sword. At the bottom of this section is the crest of 881 Squadron of the Fleet Air Arm and the words "In memory of Lt Cdr DRB Cosh, DSC, RCNVR, commanding officer of 881 Squadron November 1943 to June 1944". The purpose of this window is absolutely clear, and was donated by the members of 881 Squadron. The window is in addition to Lt Commander Cosh's CWGC headstone, which is in the section of St Gregory's Churchyard set aside for Commonwealth War Graves.

Lieutenant-Commander Digby Rex Bell Cosh, was obviously held in great esteem by those he commanded. He is described by ex-Petty Officer Jack Deeble, an aircraft radio mechanic aboard the aircraft carrier HMS Pursuer, as being "a perfect gentleman who treated everybody fairly". But even more than this is the fact that he is the only airman buried in a Border cemetery, who commanded an operational combat unit, and who additionally had gained a gallantry award.

DRB Cosh was born in the Province of Ontario, Canada on 11th September 1918. He joined the Canadian Navy, as a reservist on the 19th June 1937, reaching the rank of Acting Sub-Lieutenant by June 1939. His full enlistment into the RCN was on 12th October 1939, when his rank of Sub-Lieutenant became permanent. Promoted to Lieutenant on the 28th May 1940, he was sent to Britain arriving on 20th August 1940. His duties between then and the 21st July 1941 are not recorded, but on that date he was posted to HMS Daedalus (i e.Lee-on-Solent airfield). He started his flying training at 24 EFTS Luton on the 11th August 1941, and completed his flying training at 1 EFTS Netheravon, after being posted there on the 29th September 1941. The date of him being awarded his "wings" is not recorded, but on the 1st March 1942 he was posted to HMS Heron for Fleet Flying Duties and a fighter course, suggesting that he had acquired his wings by that date. On the 15th July 1942 he was posted to 892 Squadron, but was quickly moved on to 890 Squadron early in September 1942. It is believed that at this time this squadron was shore based, but on the 14th June 1943 the Squadron embarked on HMS Illustrious. He was transferred to 893

Squadron serving on HMS Formidable, and was promoted to Lieutenant Commander on the 3rd November 1943. A week later he was appointed Commanding Officer of 881 Squadron. This squadron had originally been formed at Lee-on-Solent in 1941, and completed several operational tours on board Fleet aircraft carriers. In August 1943 the squadron swapped its Grumman Martlett II's for Grumman Wildcat V's (essentially the same aircraft, but with a more powerful engine and a new name - actually the name by which it was known, both by the American company who designed it and the US Navy). This was a dumpy, stubby fighter specifically designed for use on aircraft carriers, and although it did not have an outstanding turn of speed, it was very manoeuvrable. Unlike British produced carrier based fighter aircraft, which were all modifications of land based versions, it had a very strong undercarriage, an essential feature for an aircraft whose landing surface could be rising and falling quite considerably. On the 7th November 1943 the Squadron became part of the 7th Naval Fighter Wing, and was embarked on the Escort aircraft carrier HMS Pursuer. This class of Escort carrier was basically a cargo ship (in fact a Liberty ship) with a flight deck fitted, and was built in America. They were particularly useful as they joined the Escorts for convoys (hence their name), providing much needed air cover. And it was on "Pursuer" that Lieutenant Commander Cosh joined the squadron on 11th November 1943.

At the beginning of February 1944 HMS Pursuer, whose commanding officer was Captain HR Graham, was detailed to become part of the escort for convoy KMS41. The escort ships which included the frigates HMS's Rochester, Scarborough, Tavy, Londonderry and Tees and the Corvettes HMS's Geranium, Mignonette and Aquamarine assembled at Donegal Mountain and the convoy formed off the Island of Oversay. There were 65 merchant ships in all, 17 bound for Freemantle and 48 bound for Gibraltar. The 17 ships bound for Freemantle were part of convoy OS67, but this was sailing in conjunction with KMS41 as far as Gibraltar. Overall command of the merchant ships was the responsibility of Sir C Ramsey sailing in the merchant ship "Silverlarch".

By mid afternoon on the 12th February the convoy was 380 miles west of Cape Finisterre. Up until that time the

**Escort Carrier HMS Pursuer. (Photo: Jack Deeble).**

convoy's progress had been without incident. Then an enemy aircraft, a Ju 290, was spotted. These were long range reconnaissance aircraft, but also carried some armament, and therefore posed a threat. As a result some fighters were launched by HMS Pursuer. The enemy aircraft was driven away by the action of these fighters, but its crew must have sent off a signal reporting the position of the convoy, because in the fading light just before sunset 7 more enemy aircraft appeared. They posed a much more serious threat to the convoy, as they were He177s and FW 200s, both of which could carry a large amount of armaments.

Although fully aware that if fighters were flown off the carrier at this time, they would have no option but to land in the near darkness, Lt. Commander Cosh decided that the risk of an attack on the convoy by the enemy aircraft was so great, that he was compelled to "fly-off" some fighters. Led by himself, 4 Wildcats took off from the "Pursuer". The other three aircraft were flown by Sub-Lieutenant TLM Brander, RNVR, Sub-Lieutenant NK Turner, RNVR and Lieutenant HP Wilson, RCNVR. They engaged the enemy aircraft, shooting down two and damaging one, the remainder fleeing for safety. But by now it was nearly dark, and the problem of getting the Wildcats, and more importantly their pilots, back on board "Pursuer" safely, had yet to be overcome. Lt-Commander Cosh used his R/T to communicate with the ship, and arrange for a makeshift flarepath to be set up on the flight deck.

**L to R. Cdr Oliphant, Officer in charge of Flight Deck, HMS Pusuer, Lt Wilson RCNVR, Lt Cdr Cosh RCNVR, Sub Lt Martin RNZNVR, Sub Lt Perrett RNZNVR.     (Photo: Jack Deeble).**

One by one the Wildcats approached and eventually all four landed on safely. As each one touched down, a loud cheer went up from the carrier's crew. Petty Officer Jack Deeble was both proud and relieved that the aircraft radios, for which he was responsible, had remained serviceable throughout the incident, and allowed the pilots to be talked down. This was one of the first, if not the first occasion, when aircraft had been landed on to an aircraft carrier during darkness. For the destruction of the enemy aircraft and the generally dangerous nature of the action, both Sub-Lieutenant Brander and Sub-Lieutenant Turner were awarded the Distinguished Service Cross, while Lieutenant Wilson and Lieutenant Commander Cosh were "Mentioned in Despatches".

HMS Pursuer returned to the UK from Gibraltar with the next homeward bound convoy. It then sailed up to Scapa Flow to start training for an attack on the German battleship "Tirpitz". This operation was to be code named "Tungsten". The "Tirpitz" had been attacked by British midget submarines in September 1943, but by early 1944 intelligence reports suggested that the damage

**Grumman Wildcat taking off from HMS Pursuer. This is the aircraft which Cosh flew in operation Tungsten.**
**(Photo: Jack Deeble).**

**Flight deck of HMS Pursuer with Wildcats of 881 Squadron.**
**(Photo: Jack Deeble).**

they had caused had been repaired, and the giant battleship was ready to put to sea. She would be a huge threat to Allied shipping, and the Admiralty decided that another attack on her was called for. A task force including two Fleet aircraft carriers and four escort aircraft carriers would sail to within aircraft striking range of Altenfjord, Norway. Once there, Barracuda torpedo bombers escorted by Wildcat, Hellcat and Corsair fighters would be flown off the carriers and attack the Tirpitz.

Shortly before "Operation Tungsten" was scheduled to take place, a full scale dress rehearsal was carried out on a mock-up at Loch Eriboll.

The departure of the task force was synchronised with that of a North Russia bound convoy, JW 58 from Loch Ewe on 27th March 1944. The Royal Navy were taking no chances, and the task force consisted of one battleship, HMS Anson, the fleet carriers, "Victorious" and "Furious", the escort carriers "Emperor", "Searcher", "Pursuer" and "Fencer", the cruisers, "Royalist", "Jamaica", "Belfast" and "Sheffield", the fleet oilers "Brown Ranger" and "Blue Ranger" plus 14 destroyers. The operation was in overall command of Vice Admiral Sir Henry Moore.

The main fleet capital ships were capable of far higher speeds than the escort carriers, and in order to keep up the escort carriers had to be steamed at their maximum speed of 17 knots throughout the operation. However, at 06.50 on the 2nd April, this was nearly the undoing of the operation, when "Pursuer's" steering gear failed as a result of this high speed, and a nasty incident was only narrowly avoided when the visibility fell to zero immediately afterwards.

The fault was repaired, and at 04.15 on the 3rd April the first wave of aircraft, consisting of 20 Barracudas and 45 fighters took off from the carriers. The second wave of aircraft consisting of 19 Barracudas and 45 fighters took off at 05.37. The fighters involved in the attack were under the overall command of Lieutenant Commander JW Sleigh from the "Pursuer". Lieutenant Commander Cosh was not only the Squadron commander, but also led Yellow section into action. He took off in Wildcat JV356 from the "Pursuer" at 04.22. The Wildcats were flown with long-range tanks, which were dropped over Loppen Island. On reaching the target Yellow Section, led by Cosh, swooped to low level, strafing the armed trawlers and armed merchantmen anchored close to the "Tirpitz". They also attacked shore based anti-aircraft batteries, and the crews of the Barracudas later reported that this had been significant in reducing the effectiveness of the AA gunnery, and had lifted their morale considerably. Lieutenant Commander Cosh resolutely took on the light AA on the stern of the "Tirpitz", and drew fire away from the attacking Barracudas. Fortunately no enemy aircraft were encountered. Cosh landed back on "Pursuer" at 06.17 hours. He had fired 710 rounds of 0.5inch ammunition even though one (1) gun had a stoppage (Wildcats were equipped with four 0.5inch Browning machine guns). All aircraft, apart from one Barracuda, had returned to their parent ships by 07.58, and the task force turned and steamed for home, arriving at Scapa Flow at 16.30 on the 6th April. The attack had been a success and much damage had been inflicted on the "Tirpitz". However, she was not mortally wounded, and this was in part due to the fact that the fighters had done their job so well. This had encouraged the Barracudas to fly lower than had been intended, and the 1600lb bombs they were using would only pierce the armoured decking of the "Tirpitz," if dropped from an altitude of greater than 3000 feet, so many of the bombs exploded fairly harmlessly against the outside of the armour plating. Lieutenant Commander Cosh was recommended to receive a Distinguished Service Cross for his part in this attack immediately on his return to Scapa Flow. The award of this medal was "Gazetted" on the 30th May. But he was destined not to receive it personally.

HMS Pursuer, after another brief foray into Norwegian waters to carry out air strikes on German shipping, returned to the mundane task of escorting convoys. Its resident Squadron, 881, had brief spells away from the ship, and disembarked to become shore based at Eglinton on the 20th June, the same day on which Lieutenant Commander Cosh joined No. 7 Course at the FLS, Milfield.

Four days later on Saturday 24th June, he took off from Milfield in Spitfire Vb EN794 coded OU-J to make simulated attacks on the North Dive Screen at Doddington, and then at the Goswick Ranges. At 11.45 the Spitfire failed to recover from a manoeuvre, which

Memorial window for Lt cdr Cosh in St. Gregory's Church, Kirknewton. (Photo: The Author).

Detail of lower section of Lt Cdr Cosh memorial window. (Photo: The Author).

it had attempted in order to make an attack on the Goswick Range, and crashed. Lieutenant Commander Cosh was killed instantly.

His funeral took place at St Gregory's Church, Kirknewton at 14.20 hours on Tuesday 27th June, and was attended by all the naval personnel serving at Milfield.

The news of his death came as a stunning shock to 881 Squadron. The second-in-command, Lieutenant Wilson is reported to have been almost inconsolable in his grief. Apart from Jack Deeble, an Alnwick man, none of the Squadron knew where Kirknewton was. But Jack explained where it was, and such was the respect in which Lieutenant Commander Cosh had been held, it was decided that the

Squadron would put the window in place.

Digby Rex Bell's Distinguished Service Cross was sent to his wife, Joan, in Canada.

## FLYING OFFICER F KURPIEL RAFVR 06/10/1944

Yet again a mid-air collision was to be the cause of several airmen's tragic deaths, including that of Flying Officer Franciszek Kurpiel. Perhaps it is a measure of how busy the skies above North Northumberland had become in that this collision was not between two fast moving fighter aircraft, but between two relatively slow twin engined training aircraft.

On Friday 6th October 1944, Flying Officer Kurpiel was a member of the crew of Anson EF806 of 62 OTU, RAF Ouston. He was a pupil Radio Navigator and alongside him in the aircraft were the pilot, Flight Sergeant RAH Stephenson, Radio Navigator Instructor, Warrant Officer VAJ Woodward, and another Radio Navigator Pupil, Pilot Officer RTF Collins, RCAF. At about 13.45, when they had been in the air for about twenty minutes, they collided with Anson W2632 of 4 AGS, RAF Morpeth. The collision occurred near Ponteland, with EF 806 coming to earth one mile east of Milbourne, whilst W2632 crashed at Higham Dykes, one mile east of the crash site of EF806. All of the crew of the 62 OTU Anson, including Flying Officer Kurpiel, were killed, as were Flight Sergeant EW Tranmere and Warrant Officer JE Restell, the pilot and pupil respectively of W2632 of 4 AGS.

Flying Officer Kurpiel, who was 36 years of age, was buried at Chevington on Wednesday 11th October 1944. The funeral service was conducted by Squadron Leader A. Stopa, the Polish Roman Catholic Chaplain for 4 AGS at RAF Morpeth.

Squadron Leader JC Hay of the Air Ministry Accident Investigation Branch, arrived at RAF Morpeth on Saturday 14th October, in connection with this accident.

## FLYING OFFICER M.E. SAUZIER RAFVR 14/10/1944

The idyllic Indian Ocean island of Mauritius was the birthplace and home of Maurice Emile Sauzier. He was born at Curcpipe on the 1st August 1920, and enlisted in the RAF on the 16th September 1941. By this time his family lived at Forest Side.

That a young man from an Island Community, which was not under any direct threat from any of the belligerents, should volunteer to serve, demonstrates the commitment of the youth of the free world to overcome the evil and tyrannical regimes which menaced.

Flying Officer Sauzier's progress through the RAF is not known, but by October 1944 he was serving at 57 OTU Eshott. On Saturday the 14th October, he was engaged in some air to ground firing practice at Druridge Bay. He was flying Spitfire V EE716. However, after making a low pass, he failed to recover control, and the aircraft crashed into a sandbank, killing him instantly.

Having paid the ultimate price for freedom, Maurice Emile Sauzier was laid to rest in Chevington Cemetery.


## FLYING OFFICER F.E. LARKMAN, RCAF 03/03/1945

Frank Ernest Larkman became the last Dominion airman to lose his life, and be buried in the Borders.

A native of Toronto, he enlisted in the RCAF there on the 15th April 1943. After being posted to several manning depots and initial training schools, he finally started his training as a navigator at 7 Air Observation School at Portage la Prairie on the 17th October 1943. He joined the RCAF as an airman in the ranks, but on the 10th March 1944 he was commissioned as a Pilot Officer. A fortnight later on 24th March he was transferred to the Air Gunners Training School at Maitland, Nova Scotia. Although it is known that he left Maitland on the 29th April 1944, there is no record of his further movements, until the report of the accident

126

in which he lost his life, whilst serving with 54 OTU at Charterhall on the 3rd March 1945. He had passed through 3 PRC at Bournemouth, but no dates of either his arrival or departure from that establishment are recorded.

On Saturday 3rd March 1945, a Beaufighter VI, KV976 took off from Charterhall to carry out an Advanced Airborne Interception Demonstration for the benefit of the two pupil crew on board. These were Pilot Officer JA Patterson RCAF, Pupil Pilot and Flying Officer FE Larkman, Pupil Navigator/Radar Operator. Their instructors were Warrant Officer PJ O'Malley as Pilot and Flight Sergeant RM Wedgewood as Navigator. It was mid-afternoon and the aircraft had reached 5,000 feet as it flew out over the sea at Lamberton just north of Berwick. At 15.14 while the aircraft was in cloud, the vacuum pump, which provided the suction for the flying instruments, failed. The loss of these vital instruments in cloud resulted in the pilot losing control, and the aircraft turned on to its back and crashed into the sea. However, the event had been witnessed by local fishing boats, which observed that three parachutes had appeared from the crashing aircraft. The fishing boat "White Heather" found both the instructor and pupil pilots, who were slightly injured, and landed them at Eyemouth. The Eyemouth lifeboat under the command of Coxswain John Jamieson also went to the scene, and recovered the body of Flight Sergeant Wedgewood, which was brought into Burnmouth. Flying Officer Larkman's body was found some time later by a fishing boat, whose identity was not recorded, and landed at Berwick.

It is assumed that Pilot Officer Patterson was at the controls, when the mishap occurred. Although a very experienced pilot with 1945 hours of flying to his credit, he had only completed 29 hours flying a Beaufighter. The layout of the cockpit area of the Beaufighter would have made it impossible for Warrant Officer O'Malley, as Instructor, to have taken the controls once the aircraft had turned on to its back, and the crash became inevitable.

The Beaufighter had claimed two more victims, and yet another Canadian was laid to rest in Fogo Churchyard.

# WHY?

"Here dead we lie because we did not choose

To live and shame the land from which we sprung.

Life, to be sure, is nothing much to lose;

But young men think it is, and we were young."

A.E. Housman


Was there any common cause of these young men's sad demise? Only one suggests itself, and although it may be trite, it is also true. And that is, because they were here.

All airmen who served as aircrew in the RAF, RAFVR and the Dominion Air Forces did so as volunteers. It is true that many of the Dominion airmen would have been conscripted into one of the services anyway, but they chose to accept an above normal risk, before they need have done so. As for the airmen from the Colonies and occupied countries, there was nothing which compelled them to serve in any branch of the services, let alone to be aircrew. So all these men were here of their own volition, when there was nothing that compelled them to be. So, yes, they died here, because by their own choice, they were here. And of course it must not be forgotten that two of the RCAF casualties were in fact American citizens, and that the USA was a neutral (i.e. non-belligerent) country, when they volunteered for service.

There is a certain amount of irony in the fact that these young men came from all corners of the world, often from remote and isolated communities, to die and be buried in relatively remote and isolated places.

But if one is looking for the causes of the air accidents, then there were several factors, which were implicated on a regular basis.

The chief one among these was inexperience. Many of the young men, who lost their lives whilst flying from Milfield, Eshott, and Charterhall had very little experience of the aircraft type they were flying, and hence had only a scant knowledge of what to do in the event of something untoward happening. Even Lieutenant Commander Cosh, although a fully operational pilot  with combat experience, would not have been very familiar with flying a Spitfire at the time he lost his life, having only been at Milfield for four days. Furthermore the flying characteristics of a Wildcat and a Spitfire would have been entirely different, and so to be attempting a low level bombing run in a Spitfire would have been a totally new experience. In the modern RAF it takes a minimum of eight weeks to convert a pilot from flying one type of aircraft to another. And that is only to acquire basic handling skills in flying the aircraft, and does not include combat manoeuvres.

Some of the Hurricane crashes at Milfield were undoubtedly caused by fuel starvation of the engine. The Merlin engine, although an excellent and well engineered power-plant, had a propensity to catch fire shortly after start-up, if it was over-primed - and by all accounts it was quite easy to over-prime it. In order that the risk to the pilot was kept to a minimum, the engine was started with the fuel supply switched to the reserve tank, which only contained a small amount of fuel. If there were to be a fire, then its intensity and duration would be reduced. But once the aircraft was airborne, the fuel supply had to be switched to the main tank. This was a procedure many of the young trainee pilots forgot, sometimes with tragic results.

The numerous mid-air collisions are perhaps a little more understandable as all but one of the victims of these accidents were training to be fighter pilots, and would therefore be involved in manoeuvres which put them close to other aircraft, which themselves were performing similar manoeuvres. But once again inexperience may have led to misjudgement of closing speeds, and the distances between aircraft, which together with the exuberance and perhaps over-confidence of youth, led to errors being made.

Six of the airmen in this guide died as a result of a crash on high ground. In most, but not all of these incidents poor weather was a factor, which contributed to the crash, and was not helped by the less than exact naviational techniques and poor equipment of the time. In fact, many other Commonwealth and exiled airmen lost their lives on the high ground of the Borders, but are not included in this guide, as they are not buried here. But their loss was attributed to these same factors.

The crew of the Whitley, which crashed at the incomplete Brunton airfield were desperately unlucky. Once again the poor weather conditions, and perhaps the lack of a navigator, had caused them to become lost in the first place, but then they had done everything correctly and made a safe landing. The ensuing collisions on take-off were just bad luck. But one can argue that ultimately the weather was to blame, because if it had not been poor, the initial landing would not have been made.

A few of the accidents happened as a result of mechanical problems, in particular engine failure, and once again it is possible that with more experience the unfortunate victims of these incidents may have been able to cope with the failure more competently.

Of the forty five airmen listed in this guide, eleven lost their lives whilst flying in a Beaufighter. There can be little doubt that the extremely poor slow speed handling characteristics of the Beaufighter, especially on the ground, were a major factor in this appalling statistic.

These faults were exaggerated in the Merlin engined Beaufighter, with which both 54 OTU at Charterhall and 409 Squadron at Acklington were equipped. In fact this version was basically underpowered, and if an engine failed during a critical phase of flight e.g. take-off, landing or a slow speed manoeuvre, the aircraft became very difficult to handle, and a crash usually resulted. Even the later Hercules engined versions did not lose this trait completely, and the throttles had to be opened with extreme caution if a swing were not to be initiated. Such was the reputation of the Beaufighter, that even the instructors seemed to be in awe of it.

When a pupil pilot was about to make his first flight in a Beaufighter he stood on the step behind the pilot's seat while the instructor took-off, made two circuits and landings, there being no facilities for dual controls. The pupil and instructor then changed places and the pupil carried out two take offs, circuits and landings, with the instructor standing behind him. In the event of anything going wrong the instructor could offer advice, but could not physically do anything as the cockpit area was too cramped. Having successfully completed two circuits the instructor left the aircraft and the pupil carried out another or more circuits alone. The inherent danger in this stage of the pupil's tuition is emphasised by the fact that the navigator/radar operator, who had been teamed up with the pilot, was not allowed to be in the aircraft at this time.

Although the Beaufighter had this unfortunate handling characteristic, it was a fine aircraft in every other respect, being an excellent weapons platform when operating at normal speeds. It was also an immensely strong aircraft, and were it not for this factor, the list of fatalities might have been even longer.

But perhaps the most bizarre cause of an accident was that which resulted in the death of "Jaap" Van Hamel. When 322 Squadron moved into Acklington to convert to the Mark XIV Spitfire, it had difficulties in getting supplies of many items necessary for the flying programme. The shortage of Coffman starter cartridges has already been mentioned. However, because one of the attributes of this new mark of Spitfire was the ability to fly at very high altitude, large amounts of oxygen were needed. And sufficient quantities were not available through the normal RAF channels, so it was "borrowed" from local hospitals. Unfortunately medical oxygen did not have all the moisture removed from it, as did aviation oxygen. Hence, when the new Spitfires reached 40,000 feet, the extremely low temperatures at that altitude (colder than -60 degrees Celsius) turned this tiny amount of moisture into ice crystals, which blocked the minute canals in the diffuser mechanism, thus starving the pilot of his oxygen supply. After some time the cause of the oxygen supply problems in 322 Squadron's Mark XIV Spitfires was discovered, but not until after "Jaap" Van Hamel had already lost his life.

It is difficult to comprehend the anguish and grief, which must have been felt by the relatives and loved ones of these unfortunate young men, which was exacerbated by the fact that they had died so far away, and often having not seen them for a long period of time. The words inscribed on Sergeant Rutherford's headstone, and requested by his mother, perhaps go some way to summing up those feelings:

"To the world, an airman,
To me, the world."

These young men's memorials do, however, serve a purpose greater than just being the marker of a grave. Collectively, they constantly remind us of the tragedy and futility of war, and that it is totally indiscriminate in its choice of victims. Perhaps they should also remind us of the generosity of the human spirit, and that we should be eternally grateful for the sacrifices made. These young men did not "give their lives", as the much misused cliche would have it, but had their lives wrenched from them.

"We know you died that we might see again

A host of Springtimes in this quiet lane"

From "Killed in Action" by Myfanwy Haycock 1942

# APPENDIX 1

Commonwealth and exiled airmen who lost their lives in the area but who are not buried in the area

**Name      Unit      Aircraft      Date**
**Place of burial**
Pilot Officer Hakam Chand Mehta
            43 Squadron  Hurricane Z3150   3rd November, 1941
Cremated. (Royal Indian Airforce)

Sergeant D Fraser
            59 OTU      Hurricane N2428   12th  June 1942
Dalston Road Cemetery, Carlisle. (RNZAF)

Sergeant H.R.E. Moureaux
            57 OTU      Spitfire R7202     3rd February 1943
Not known but probably repatriated to France. (Free French Airforce)

Not known. (RNZAF)
#Crew of Wellington R1535, GR-G of 301  (Polish Squadron),
                                        9th January 1943

        Flying Officer T.Tyrala
        Flying Officer T. Sokolinskin
        Sergeant J. Pasierski
        Sergeant E. Tabacznski
                All buried in Polish war Cemetery Newark.

* Sergeant H.R.E. Moureaux
            57 OTU      Spitfire R7202     3rd February 1943
Not known but probably repatriated to France (Free French Air Force)

Pilot Officer Neve de Meterginer
            57 OTU      Spitfire P8528     9th April 1943
Not known but probably repatriated to France (Free French Air Force)

Flight Sergeant H.A. De Freitas
             59 OTU        Hurricane AGIII  5th May 1943
Perth (Scotland) Cemetery (RAAF)

# Sergeant S. Zawilinski
             4 AGS         Botha L6531       10th May 1943
Morpeth Parish Church

Flight Sergeant C.F. Clements
             57 OTU        Spitfire R6813    7th July 1943
Not known (RNZAF)

Flying Officer R. Van de Poll
             350 Squadron  Spitfire BM 399   11th July 1943
Repatriated to Belgium (Belgian)

Sergeant Grawel
             350 Squadron  Spitfire EN 860   11th July 1943
Repatriated to Belgium (Belgian)

Flight Sergeant E.W. Mills
             57 OTU        Spitfire K9953    7th October 1943
Not known (RCAF)

Sergeant D. Demades
             57 OTU        Spitfire R7063    11th October 1943
Not known but probably repatriated to France (Free French Air Force)

Pilot Officer E.A. Merkley
             57 OTU        Spitfire K9824(XO-V) 19th November 1943

Not known (RCAF)

* Crew of Lancaster DS650 1666 HCU 3rd March 1944
             Pilot Officer R.G. Calder(RCAF)
                          Edinburgh (Morningside) Cemetery
             Flight Sergeant R.W. Campbell (RCAF)
                          Stonefall Cemetery, Harrogate
             Warrant Officer 2 F.J. Leech (RCAF)
                          Stonefall Cemetery
             Sergeant J. Simms (RCAF)
                          Stonefall Cemetery

Sergeant W.A. Lynn
          57 OTU        Spitfire X4595        17th March 1944
Not known (RAAF)

# Crew of Beaufighter EL 457 132 OTU 15th May 1944
          Flying Officer G.A.E. Malchair (Belgian)
                    Repatriated to Belgium
          Flight Sergeant R.L.A. Closen (Belgian)
                    Repatriated to Belgium

*Pilot Officer J.C. Lees (RCAF)
          434 Squadron  Halifax MZ908(WL-O)  19th September
1944
Stonefall Cemetery

# Crew of Stirling EE972(OG-C)  1665 HCU  25th September 1944
          Flight Sergeant P.S. Coronel (RAAF)
                    Stonefall Cemetery

# Crew of Lancaster KB745 VR-V 4th October 1944
          Flying Officer G.R. Duncan (RCAF)
                    Stonefall Cemetery
          Flying Officer W.G. Layng (RCAF)
                    Stonefall Cemetery
          Flying Officer A. Gaddass (RCAF)
                    Stonefall Cemetery
          Sergeant M.R. Karstens (RCAF)
                    Stonefall Cemetery
          Sergeant D.A. Trott (RCAF)
                    Stonefall Cemetery
          Sergeant T.B. Tiernay (RCAF)
                    Parkestone Cemetery, Poole

Pilot Officer R.T.F. Collins
          62 OTU        Anson EF806        6th October 1944
Stonefall Cemetery (RCAF)

Pilot Officer N.L. Gordon
          56 OTU        Typhoon RB343        st February 1945
Springbank Cemetery, Aberdeen (RCAF)

# Crew of Halifax NR126 (PT-X) 420 Squadron 17th February 1945
     Flying Officer M.B. Stock (RCAF)
        Stonefall Cemetery
     Flying Officer R.B. Trout (RCAF)
        Stonefall Cemetery
     Flying Officer R.A. Floripe (RCAF — USA)
        Stonefall Cemetery
     Pilot Officer T.L. O'Kane (RCAF)
        Stonefall Cemetery
     Flying Officer D.L. Neil (RCAF)
        Stonefall Cemetery

Flying Officer P.N. Bernhart
     56 OTU     Tempest NV924    3rd March 1945
Stonefall Cemetery (RCAF)

Flying Officer R.F.D. Smith
     56 OTU     Typhoon MP187   8th March 1945
Stonefall Cemetery (RCAF) (USA)

Flying Officer G.A. Sullivan
     56 OTU     Typhoon EK364   27th March 1945
Stonefall Cemetery (RCAF)

The area in which these incidents took place is the whole of the county of Northumberland north of the River Wansbeck plus the old counties of Roxburghshire and Berwickshire.

The list, although exhaustive, should not be regarded as definitive.

The stories of incidents involving casualties marked # are told in ``Where the Hills Meet the Sky'' while those marked * are told in ``A Border Too High'', both books being compiled by the author of this guide.

# APPENDIX II

Luftwaffe airmen who lost their lives in the area

Crew of He 111 1H + HL of 3/KG26 3rd February 1940
Lt L. von Bru\dning
Fw H. Panzlaff
Lffz W. Remischke— All buried Chevington Cemetery
Fw H. Peterson— missing, believed killed

Crew of He 111 of 2/KG2627th February 1940
Hptm J. Helm
Uffz K. Lassig— Both buried Chevington Cemetery
Uffz H. Buchisch
Ofw A. Thiele
Gefr W. Rixen— All missing, believed killed

Crew of Ju 88 4D + AD of 6/KG3029th March 1940
Oblt R. Quadt
Fw G. Hartung
Uffz E. Hesse
? A. Wunderling— All buried Chevington Cemetery

Crew of Me 110 of 1/2G7615th August 1940
Obltn Loobes
Uffz Brock— Both believed killed but ultimate fate unknown

Crew of Me 110 of 3/ZG7615th August 1940
Ltn Koehter
Uffz Oelsner— Both believed killed but ultimate fate unknown

Crew of Me 110 M8 + EK of 2/2G7615th August 1940
Obgfr K. Lenk— missing, believed killed

Crew of Ju 88 M2 + JL of 3/KFG10613th March 1941
Ltn Z.Z.R. Dietze
Obgfr W. Wesseres
Obgfr H. Vandamme— All missing
Ltn H. Voigtlander-Tetzner— Thornaby-on-Tees Cemetery

Crew of Ju 88 S4 + JH of 1/KFG 50630th April/1st May 1941
Lt H. Jark
Fw K. Pahneke
Uffz J. Schaare— All missing
Obgfr J. Schumacher— Brandesburton churchyard, near Hornsea,
Yorks (body washed up from the sea)

* Crew of Ju 88, VB + KM of 2 Staffel Ob.d.L.28th May 1941
Lt F. Gortam
Gfr H. Matthius— Both buried Cannock Chase German War Cemetery
after initially having been buried at Jedburgh

Crew of Ju 88 4D + DB of StabIII/KG301st September 1941
Obfw H. Riede
Obltn R. Elle
Obfw H. Dorn
Fw W. Muller— All buried Chevington Cemetery

*# Crew of Do 217 U5 + DL of 1/KG225th March 1943
Obfw F. Kalbfleisch— Were buried in St Gregory's Churchyard,
Kirknewton.
Gefr K. Lahr. But now with the exception of
Uffz F. Freyhall, Uffz W. Frankare buried at Cannock Chase

*# Crew of Do 217 U5 + KP of IV/KG225th March 1943
HptmR. Frase
Uffz W. Schneider
Uffz A. Ille— All buried Dalston Road Cemetery, Carlisle
Gefr S. Hartz— killed but place of burial not known

*# Crew of Ju 88, 3E + BH of 1/KG625th March 1943
Obfw F. Lang
Uffz W. Schulz
Obfw K. Kleih
Gefr W. Fiedler— All buried in Chevington Cemetery

*# Crew of Ju 88 3E + MN of II/KG625th March 1943
Obltn P. Rogge
Uffz E. Glick
Uffz K. Brinkman
Uffz W. Walter— initially all buried at Fogo Church, now all buried at
Cannock Chase

As with Appendix I casualties marked # and * have their stories included in ``Where the Hills Meet the Sky'' and ``A Border Too High'' respectively.

Abbreviations of rank with British equivalent
Hptm—Hauptman=(Flight Lieutenant)
Obltn—Oberleutnant=Captain (Flying Officer)
Ltn—Leutnant=Lieutenant (Pilot Officer)
Uffgz—Unteroffiziere=(Corporal)
Obfw—Obersfeldwebel= (Flight Sergeant)
Fw—Feldwebel=Corporal (Sergeant)
Obgfr—Obersgefreiter=Lance-Corporal (LAC)
Gfr—Gefreiter=Private (ACl)

# APPENDIX III

Commonwealth and other non-British casualties who were not airmen buried in the Borders

L. MackenzieBritish Honduras Forestry Unit6th September 1943

E.E. RobinsonBritish Honduras Forestry Unit17th April 1944

Both of these men were in the area to replace those forestry workers who had joined the armed forces. There was a significant number of such men in the Border area with a large group centred around Duns. It is believed that both of these men died of natural causes.

Edoardo PirraginoItalian P.O.W. No. 2376313th September 1943

All three men are buried in Duns Cemetery

# BIBLIOGRAPHY

Brown, A. - "Airmen in Exile" - Sutton Publishing 2000

Bruin, J and Van der Werff, J. - "Vrijheid achter de horizon" Van Reemst Uitgeverij 1998

Clark, P. - "Where the Hills Meet the Sky" (2nd Edition) Glen Graphics 1998

Clark, P. - "A Border Too High" - Glen Graphics 1999

Delvc, K. - "Source Book of the RAF" - Airlife 1994

Evans, A. - "Milfield, not just an airfield" - Oxford Instant Printing Service 1994

Huisman Van Bergen, A. - "De Vervolgden" - Boom 1999

Jefford, C.G. - "RAF Squadrons" - Airlife 1988

Lake, A. - "Flying Units of the RAF" - Airlife 1999

Milberry, L. and Halliday, H. - "The Royal Canadian Air Force at War 1939-1945" - Canav Books 1990

Moyle, H. - "The Hampden File" - Air Britain 1989

Powell, A. (Editor) - "Shadows of War" - Sutton Publishing 1999

   (A collection of Women's Poetry from World War II)

Thompson, J.B. - "Charterhall Story" - Air Research 1995

Walton, D. - "Northumberland Aviation Diary" - Norav Publications 1999

# SOURCES

**Public Record Office (PRO), Kew**

| | | |
|---|---|---|
| AIR16/780 | - | Records of Typhoon conversion unit, Milfield |
| AIR16/800 | - | FLS records |
| AIR27/142 | - | ORB, 10 Squadron |
| AIR27/441 | - | ORB, 43 Squadron |
| AIR27/543,544 | - | ORB, 58 Squadron |
| AIR27/686 | - | ORB, 83 Squadron |
| AIR27/914 | - | ORB, 121 Squadron |
| AIR27/1009, 1010- | | ORB, 150 Squadron |
| AIR27/1138 | - | ORB, 184 Squadron |
| AIR27/1372 | - | ORB, 222 Squadron |
| AIR27/1471 | - | ORB, 242 Squadron |
| AIR27/1481 | - | ORB, 245 Squadron |
| AIR27/1511 | - | ORB, 253 Squadron |
| AIR27/1716 | - | ORB, 322 Squadron |
| AIR27/1791 | - | ORB, 406 Squadron |
| AIR27/1802 | - | ORB, 410 Squadron |
| AIR28/17 | - | ORB, RAF Acklington |
| AIR28/450 | - | ORB, RAF Leeming |
| AIR28/481 | - | ORB,RAF Linton-on-Ouse |

| | | |
|---|---|---|
| AIR28/681 | - | ORB, RAF Scampton |
| AIR28/717 | - | ORB, RAF Snaith |
| AIR28/870 | - | ORB, RAF Usworth |
| AIR29/526 | - | ORB, Glider Pilots Exercise Unit |
| AIR29/590 | - | ORB, 4 AGS |
| AIR29/681 | - | ORB, 53 OTU |
| AIR29/682 | - | ORB, 54 OTU |
| AIR29/683 | - | ORB, 57 OTU |
| AIR29/684 | - | ORB, 59 OTU and RAF Milfield |
| AIR29/685 | - | ORB, 62 OUT |
| AVIA5/19-W749 | - | Report on Hampden L4054 |
| AVIA 5/22 - W1514 | - | Report on Spitfire P7352 |
| AVIA 5/22 - W1578 | - | Report on Hurricane P3715 |
| ADM 1/15695 - | - | Reports on Operation Tungsten |
| ADM 199/2102 - | | Reports on convoy KMS41 |

### National Archives of Australia, National Archives of Canada and New Zealand Defence Force Personnel Archives

Personal correspondence in connection with airmen's service records.

## Air Historical Branch, Ministry of Defence

Personal correspondence with regard to casualty records.


## Royal Air Force Personnel Management Agency

Personal correspondence with regard to service details of members of the RAFVR.


## Northumberland County Record Office, Morpeth

NC 9/3               Police Occurrence book for Wooler

EP 3/31 )          Correspondence between Kirknewton Church

EP 3/32 )          and Imperial War Graves Commission


## Scottish Borders Archive and Local History Centre, Selkirk

D/90/5/1          Berwickshire police records of incidents involving aircraft 1942-1945


## RAF Museum, Hendon

Form 1180 for some aircraft, where available

## Fleet Air Arm Museum, Yeovilton

Personal correspondence regarding 881 Squadron

## **The Polish Institute and Sikorski Museum**

Personal correspondence regarding Polish airmen

# INDEX

## People

### A

Achong, Mr.  92
Allworth Sgt. W.H.  42
Anderson, P.C. James  75
Anderson, Tommy  95
Andrew, F/Sgt. W.  81
Archibald, Petty Officer A.H.P. 80
Armstrong, Willy  49
Austin Pilot Officer R.S.  34

### B

Bainbridge, LAC  97
Bell, F/O R.C.  64
Beurling 'Screwball'  17
Bigmore, F/O G.W.  86
Blasinski Pilot Officer W.  32
Bonnewith, Lottie  79
Bosanquet, Mrs  70
Bouwer, Jan  98
Brander, Sub/Lt. T.L.M.  107
Brodie, Sgt. R.H.  61

Brown, F/Sgt. E.L.  66
Brown, Miss D.A.  52
Bryant Sgt P.W.  35

### C

Carey Sergeant F.  16
Collins, P/O R.T.F.  113
Comber-Higgs Pilot Officer E.D. 31
Cosh, Lt/Cmndr. D.R.B.  105
Cosson, F/Sgt. T.  74
Cosson, Miss P.  75
Currie, P/O R.J.  78

### D

Dagg, John  43
Dawson, Sgt. G.R.  72
De Man, Hugo  98
Deeble J.  6
Dixon, Sgt. M.A.  63
Donohue, F/Lt. P.A.  55
Dougal, James  80
Douglas, W/O H.A.  95

### E

Edner, P/O  91
Edwards, Sgt. E.F.  83

### F

145

146

**RAF Units & Establishments.**

Linton-on-Ouse   31
Ludham   102
Manston   91
Marham   44
Middle Wallop   91
Milfield   18
Morpeth   113
Netheravon   90
Oakington   60
Ossington   51
Ouston   113
Scampton   27
Shoreham   91
Snaith   41
South Cerney   28
Stapleford Tawney   91
Sutton Bridge   45
Swanton Morley   83
Tangmere   102
Ternhill   90
Thruxton   90
Usworth   85
Uxbridge   28
Wattisham   59
Watton   68
Westhampnett   102
Winfield   75
Woodvale   94


**Squadrons**

10   34
43   16
58   31
75   59
83   27
121   91
132   24
150   41
164   19
167   102
184   78
222   93
242   90
253   91
322   102
610   33

**Miscellaneous Units**

15 OTU   37
10 OTU   35
11 OTU   42
19 OTU   34
23 OTU   41
52 OTU   20
53 OTU   96
54 OTU   97
55 OTU   39
56 OTU   45
57 OTU   64
59 OTU   72

60 OTU   24
62 OTU   24

2(P) AFU   59
3(P) AFU   82
5(P)AFU   90
6(P)AFU   59
12(P)AFU   75
14(P)   51
17(P)AFU   68
1 EFTS, Hatfield   102
1 EFTS, Netheravon   105
2 EFTS, Worcester   71
21 EFTS, Booker   102
24 EFTS, Luton   105
1515 BATF   71
1517 BATF   82
4 AGS   113
7 AGS   60
Glider Pilot Exercise Unit   90
Specialised Low Attack School Instructors (SLAIS)   19
Fighter Leaders School (FLS)   20
48 MU   17
1655 MTU   44
3 PRC, Bournemouth   35
11 PRC, Brighton and Bournemouth   85

**RCAF Units & Establishments**

1 Manning Depot   34
3 ITS   96
5 ITS   51
3 EFTS, London (Ontario)   76
3 EFTS, Victousville   45
5 EFTS, Lethbridge   34
7 EFTS   47
10 EFTS, Mount Hope   61
11 EFTS, Cap De La Madelaine   74
16 EFTS, Edmonton   54
17 EFTS, Stanley   48
20 EFTS, Oshawa   63
1 SFTS, Camp Borden   87
2 SFTS, Uplands   96
7 SFTS, MacLeod   59
8 SFTS, Moncton   63
9 SFTS, Summerside   45
10 SFTS, Dauphin   82
12 SFTS, Brandon   41
13 SFTS, St. Hubert   74
14 SFTS Aylmer   76
41 SFTS,Moncton   88
1 AOS   76
6 AOS, Prince albert   42
3 B&GS, MacDonald   42
4 B&GS, Fingal   60
6 B&GS, Mountain View   76
1 (Fighter) OTU, Bagotville   61
AGTS, Maitland   114
7 OTU, Debert   34
Central Flying School, Trenton

37
'Y' Depot, Halifax   39

UK-based Squadrons -
406   39
410   45
Canadian-based Squadrons -
119(BR)   73

## RAAF Units & Establishments

1 ITS, Somers   58
3 ITS, Sandgate   96
5 ITS, Pearce W.A.   51
2 EFTS, Archerfield   96
3 EFTS, Essondon   58
7 EFTS, Western Junction   87
9 EFTS, Cunderdin W.A.   51
1 SFTS, Point Cook   87
2 SFTS, Wagga   96
4 SFTS, Geraldton W.A.   51
5 SFTS, Uranquinty   96
1 AOS, Cootamundra   85
3 B&GS, West Sale   85
1 Embarkation Depot, Ascot Vale
85
2 Embarkation Depot, Bradfield
Park N.S.W.   96

3 Embarkation Depot, Sandgate
96
5 Embarkation Depot, Perth W.A.
51

## RNZAF Units & Establishments

1 ITW, Levin   60
1 EFTS, Taieri   71
3 EFTS, Harewood   75
4 EFTS, Whenuapai   41
2 SFTS, Woodbourne (Blenheim)
71
3 SFTS, Wigram   75

## Other BCATP Establishments.

26 EFTS, Guinea Fowl, S.Rhodesia
67
21 SFTS, Kumalo, S.Rhodesia   67
22 SFTS, Thornhill, S.Rhodesia
67
21 PTC, Egypt   68
22 PTC, Egypt   68
2 PRU, Egypt   68

## Fleet Air Arm Units, Royal Naval Air Stations & Royal Navy Ships

HMS Daedalus (RNAS
Lee-on-Solent)   80

151

HMS Heron   105

HMSFormidable   106

HMS Pursuer   106

HMS Rochester   106

HMS Scarborough   106

HMS Tavy   106

HMS Londonderry   106

HMS Tees  106

HMS Geranium   106

HMS Mignonette   107

HMS Aquamarine   107

HMS Anson   110

HMS Victorious   110

HMS Furious   110

HMS Emperor   110

HMS Searcher   110

HMS Fencer   110

HMS Royalist   110

HMS Jamaica   110

HMS Belfast   110

HMS Sheffield   110

RFA Brown Ranger   110

RFA Blue Ranger   110

RNAS Eglinton   111

781 Squadron   80

881 Squadron   106

890 Squadron   105

892 Squadron   105

893 Squadron   106

**Note-**

RFA -Royal Fleet Auxiliary
RNAS - Royal Naval Air Station

154